"Nowell's prophetic call strikes like a hammer on the anvil of Scripture. No reader will feel entirely comfortable here, myself included. Yet alongside the ringing iron is the whisper of grace, both the wellspring and the ultimate end of all Christian service."

—Jedd Medefind, president, Christian Alliance for Orphans

"In his compelling voice, David Nowell leads readers to discover what it looks like to truly love 'the least of these' and shine the light of Christ into some of the world's darkest places. Filled with unforgettable stories from the field, Nowell's writing will both break your heart and lift your vision. This insightful book motivates every believer to act with biblical wisdom, practical actions, and compelling clarity. *Dirty Faith* is a must-read for those who want to put their faith into action by serving others."

—Dr. Erwin W. Lutzer, senior pastor, The Moody Church

"David Nowell has challenged not only our view of the Church's responsibility in light of the worldwide plague of violence on children—from poverty to homelessness to prostitution—he has challenged our view of Jesus Christ. Nowell's Jesus has dirt under his fingernails and calluses on his hands. The Word becoming flesh is not just incarnation, it is a holiness that is willing to be stained by the brokenness of a world that would abuse an innocent child. I want my staff to read this book. It will challenge them to do what is required of them, and then some."

—Dr. Walter Crouch, president/CEO,
Appalachia Service Project

DIRTY
FAITH

DIRTY FAITH

BRINGING THE LOVE OF CHRIST TO THE LEAST OF THESE

DAVID Z. NOWELL

BETHANY HOUSE PUBLISHERS
a division of Baker Publishing Group
Minneapolis, Minnesota

© 2014 by David Z. Nowell

Published by Bethany House Publishers
11400 Hampshire Avenue South
Bloomington, Minnesota 55438
www.bethanyhouse.com

Bethany House Publishers is a division of
Baker Publishing Group, Grand Rapids, Michigan

Printed in the United States of America

Library of Congress Cataloging-in-Publication Data is on file at the Library of Congress, Washington, DC.

ISBN 978-0-7642-1213-0

Some names of persons and other details have been changed to protect their privacy.

Cover design by Dan Pitts

14 15 16 17 18 19 20   7 6 5 4 3 2 1

green press
INITIATIVE

For Ileana, Carolena, Graziella, Tatiani,
Gleice, Yara, Alexandro, Calebe . . .

And the nameless, faceless millions of children
who have called the streets their home.

Contents

Contents

Introduction

One billion children in our world live in poverty. That doesn't simply mean they have no Internet access or nice homes. It's more than the fact that they are hungry or have inadequate clothing. It means they're desperate; it means they are children being sold—or selling themselves. It means some are living in prison conditions more deplorable than you can imagine. It means twenty-one thousand children die of preventable causes *every* day.[1] Twenty-one thousand children.

Our God loves every one of them deeply, passionately, and he calls us to be the hands, feet, and heart of that love. He calls *all* of us to live out his love for them.

But getting there is not easy.

A refrain you will hear consistently throughout the following pages is that there are no super-Christians, but there certainly are some folks whose lives show they take Jesus very seriously. You'll never find a super-faith, but you may find a way of living that gives evidence to the presence of faith—and grace—in our lives.

This book is about a journey—a journey of faith and grace that is transformational to both the traveler and those encountered along the path. I hope you will sojourn here with me. The journey has a backstory, and telling it is the best way to introduce you to some people and some voices you will hear throughout this book.

The story begins over two decades ago. Actually, it starts many years before that, but for our purposes, we'll start in the late 1980s. At that time, reports began to filter out of South America that street children were being murdered in their sleep in some cities of Brazil. *Newsweek* magazine featured a story, "Who Is Killing Brazil's Street Children?"[2] The answer, it turned out, was the very people charged with protecting them: the police. Throughout the '80s, Brazil had faced a growing problem with street kids. Rapid changes in society, an exploding impoverished class, a collapse of family, and, for lack of a better term, a prevailing evil all melted into a maelstrom that drove uncountable numbers of children from their homes into the streets. Some estimates placed the mark as high as five million kids living on the streets, primarily in the big cities: São Paulo, Rio de Janeiro, Campinas, Belo Horizonte.

And guess what? Kids don't last long living in that context: three to five years' life expectancy once they hit the streets.[3] They are exploited, abused, in constant danger. They are hungry, tired, afraid, angry. The boys become thieves to survive; almost all of the girls—and many of the boys—sell themselves. They all beg. By the late 1980s, the streets were populated by swarms of adolescent and preadolescent thieves, prostitutes, and beggars. Throwaway kids: filthy, disease-ridden, desperate. And yet they were all children God loves as much as he loves you and me, the kind of kids Jesus called his brothers and sisters.

These were not the kids next door; they were dangerous. Anyone on the streets was fair game for them. They harassed drivers. They snatched purses from women walking to their jobs. They robbed the patrons of shops and restaurants. *Children*

God loves as much as he loves you and me. But businessmen didn't see it that way. No, these were not children created in the image of a loving Father. They were a pestilence, vermin, and they needed to be exterminated.

What happened next is well-documented. Businessmen began to hire vigilante gangs (whom the courts later determined to be off-duty local and federal police) to "sweep" the streets at night, killing the children as they slept. Over 4,600 assassinations of children are documented. And for the most part, Brazil turned a cold shoulder to the stories. Street vermin should expect no better. The body of one boy was found with a note stuck to his chest: "He lived on the streets. He would not go to school. He had no future. He deserved to die." On July 23, 1993, a vigilante group murdered eight sleeping children on the steps of the Candelária Church in Rio; red-colored outlines of eight bodies are permanently painted near where they died.[4]

But God loves these children. And if we are followers of Jesus, not just believers, we love them, too.

Back the story up a couple more decades and meet some serious followers. In the 1960s, Presbyterian missionaries Jack and Evangel Smith took their young family to Ethiopia. With hearts overwhelmed by the needs of the ever-present children of the streets, they started a job-training program for the kids. By the time the communist regime that had deposed Haile Selassie forced them out of the country in 1977, that backyard program called Hope Enterprises had legs of its own. Today, the indigenously run and supported program annually touches the lives of over ten thousand Ethiopian children.

By 1991, when the street-kid problem in Brazil was at its peak, the Smith family was in California. Jack and Evangel's son Philip was finishing college. David Swoap, President Reagan's deputy secretary of health and human services, knew of Jack's passion to transform the lives of children at mortal risk and Philip's calling to follow the same path as his dad. While Philip was thinking of work in Mozambique, Jack challenged him to consider Brazil instead, where the situation was so dire, so critical. They could not sit idly by while children died.

God loves these children. And when he tells us to defend the fatherless—that caring for the widow and orphan is the kind of religion he approves—he also promises to go there with us, to prepare our path, to make the provision.

So Philip and Jack cashed in their frequent-flyer miles and boarded a Pan Am flight to Brazil. No funding, didn't speak Portuguese, only a little experience working with mortal-risk children, but not really a plan. Just trusting a faithful God—and passionate about caring for his children. Before they ever touched down in Brazil, a casual conversation with a fellow passenger led to the donation of an orphanage property in Campinas, a major city of 1.2 million people about an hour's drive northwest of São Paulo. The abandoned orphanage, on a thirty-five-acre property known as the City of Youth, had closed in the late 1980s after several decades of operation, but now it was theirs. Once a place where children were warehoused, it was absolutely not the vision Jack and Philip had for their program—but it was a property with buildings, with potential, with promise. But remember: no understanding of the Portuguese language, and no money.

Jack returned to the U.S. hoping to secure operational funds. Philip stayed in Brazil, picking up a few words of Portuguese every day, learning the lay of the land, and trying to discern what they would do with this incredible gift that had been dropped in their laps. But the reality was that two years of abandonment to the jungles of Brazil will do a lot of damage to any facility, and the campus of the City of Youth was no exception to the rule. A local engineering firm donated the time to develop a firm bid on the cost of bringing the facility up to code. The

14

number: $119,720, a sum far beyond the resources of the three men. Philip called Jack and David with the bad news.

But God (recurrent theme in the pages to follow) already had it all worked out.

As Isaiah puts it,

> If you do away with the yoke of oppression,
> with the pointing finger and malicious talk,
> and if you spend yourselves in behalf of the hungry
> and satisfy the needs of the oppressed,
> then your light will rise in the darkness,
> and your night will become like the noonday.
> The Lord will guide you always;
> he will satisfy your needs in a sun-scorched land
> and will strengthen your frame.
>
> Isaiah 58:9–11

If you spend yourselves. God's not interested in our passive involvement. He wants us to immerse ourselves in being servants.

God was getting serious about making provision. Menlo Park Presbyterian Church in the Bay Area of California announced that the church would make a one-time grant to one start-up missions organization. The grant amount: $120,000. Jack was invited to apply, and, from among fifty applicants, their project was selected. Hope Unlimited for Children was born, with $280 left over to start work with the kids.

Another lesson on this journey: God promises provision, not ease of travel. *Manna and quail sound like a nice dinner, but would you really want to camp out in the desert for the next forty years?*

In the spring of 1992, Philip, beginning to get command of the foreign language, opened the doors of the City of Youth to receive the first boys who would call Hope home. Street kids were given a safe place to live with lots of love, educational and vocational programming, and recreational opportunities. A beautiful setting for beautiful children. What former street child would not love a place like this?

Every boy ran away.

Hugs were not enough. These children of the street needed discipline, structure, tough love. They needed a cultural current of their peers to sweep them in the right direction. They needed more than just a bed to sleep in at night and activities to keep them busy during the day.

The great change in Hope came with the hiring of a Brazilian policeman-turned-pastor, Uélide da Silva, whose years of experience on the streets had taught him how to command the respect of tough street boys. Soon the Hope model began to take shape. The City of Youth became a place where adolescent boys learned what it means to be part of a family, acquired educational and vocational skills, and had time for play, sports, and recreation. They learned that God loves them. It became a place with rules, expectations, and consequences. Kids started staying and calling the City of Youth home.

Now, over two decades later, it is evident God has been—and is—right in the middle of this thing. That initial boys' program is still going strong, but the campus is beautifully softened by the presence of a girls' counterpart. (Wait a few chapters until you hear how God pulled that one off.) Wonderful, godly young women who come from circumstances barely imaginable. Girls sold by their mothers as prostitutes when they were twelve, ten, nine years old. Girls abused, abandoned, exploited. Commodities. Giggling teenage girls whose lives have been transformed. *Precious children of God.* And Hope Unlimited has been blessed to be the agent of God's transformation in their lives. You'll read their stories as we wind our way along this journey.

Jack passed away after a battle with cancer in 1997, and Evangel claimed her heavenly crown a decade later. David still serves as a director emeritus on Hope's board. Philip has grown from the young man running the campus to the CEO of Hope, guiding our Brazilian leadership and the organization to envision new ways to minister, to live out love for God's kids. You'll see his name a lot in these pages.

I became the president of Hope in 2007. Partnering with Philip, we lead the U.S. component of the organization. The ministry—Christian *charity* as Paul uses the word in 1 Corinthians 13—continues to grow, evolve, and mature. There have been a lot of changes in twenty-plus years. A campus in a second city. A high-quality preschool ministering to hundreds of kids—and their parents—in a slum. Community-based homes for sibling groups. A transition program for graduates that actually works; documented employment and stable-living metrics for young adults two years out of our program consistently run in the high 70 to low 80 percentiles. A one-of-its-kind-in-the-world program for incarcerated kids—Jesus meant what he said when he called prisoners his brothers and sisters; I guess that makes them our brothers and sisters, too. A graduate church that is led, funded, and populated by Hope graduates, a beacon of God's light in an evilly dark Brazilian slum—and the place where we see our Hope grandchildren beginning to take their first steps down very different paths than their parents. Mission and vision programs that help churches from around the world begin to understand what it is to be light breaking forth in the darkness.

You will meet many of the kids of Hope in the pages to follow. I wish I could take every reader to Brazil with me and let the grace of God that spills out of these young lives absolutely soak you. To protect them, I've changed their names, but their stories are faithfully told.

As part of Hope, I've been blessed to get to know Philip, David, the incredible Brazilian team led by Pastor Derli Barbosa—who pour their lives into kids the world ignores—and, of course, the kids themselves. But I've also received a greater gift: a broader glimpse of followers of Christ who are really, *really*, serious about caring for peripheral people.

But I need to be very honest with you here. We—American churches, the Church, individual believers—are not there yet. Not where we need to be. Not where the love of Christ compels us to be. Usually not even close. Remember David's words in Psalm 23? "You anoint my head with oil; my cup overflows" (v. 5)? I fear we are not overflowing, spilling the grace of God on those Jesus called the "least of these, my brothers and sisters," because the dryness, superficiality, and sterility of our faith belies our ever having had our heads anointed with the extraordinary grace that is God's giving of himself to us. Scripture does not know an arm's length faith. Look what Paul says about Jesus himself:

> Who, being in very nature God, did not consider equality with God something to be used to his own advantage; rather, he made himself nothing by taking the very nature of a servant.
>
> Philippians 2:6–7

And that is the way this faith business must work itself out in our lives. Followers of Christ become servants of others, especially those rejected by society, those living tertiary lives—the orphan, the child trafficked for her body, the child prisoner, the hungry child, the least of these.

This is a book about perspectives and possibilities. It is about looking at our world through the lens of grace, about seeing people as Christ does. It is about a different way of extending grace to and beyond the community of faith. It is about compassion—hurting alongside those in need.

But, again, it is not about a super-Christianity; I don't find that concept in the New Testament. It is about normative faith, the kind that lives out the life of Christ. The kind of faith our

18

Lord expects of every one of us. A faith that embraces what society marginalizes; the kind that finds meaning and fulfillment in servanthood. A faith that rejects entitlement, status, privilege. A faith rarely clean and never sterile. It is a faith that lives life among the least of these, my brothers and my sisters. It is the embodiment of Christ in the midst of the darkest evil of our world.

I call it dirty faith.

PART ONE

CONTEXT

Throwaway Kids
and Peripheral People

My name is Ileana.

When I was eight, my stepfather went to prison. My mother became a drug addict. We did not have much money, so she told me to go out and make some. I started collecting tin cans and other trash in the streets to recycle, but my mother always complained that I was not bringing home enough money.

One day the owner of the grocery store on the corner told me he thought I was beautiful. I told my mother, who became very quiet. That night she left the house very late, and I went to sleep before she returned. When she arrived back home, she woke me up and told me to go into the little plywood storage shed in our backyard. I did not understand, but when I got there, the grocery store owner was waiting for me, smiling and drunk. My mother asked me to

lie down on the bed, and then she left. The grocery store
owner tied my hands and feet to the old bunk bed that was
there. I started to cry and asked him what he wanted. . . .
He started to hit me, saying that I was useless, and then he
began to abuse me.

The next day I was not allowed to leave the storage shed.
I was locked up there for about three months, being abused
two or three times a week. The first time they let me out I
was terrified of everything. But then my mother stopped
taking drugs and asked for my forgiveness. But my happi-
ness did not last long. In less than two weeks the nightmare
began again. This time I don't know how long I lived like
this, being locked up for weeks at a time in the shed.

When I was thirteen, I stole some money my mother
had hidden away that she had made from my prostitution.
I ran away to my grandmother's house in São Paulo, where
I had traveled a few times with my mother. I lived with my
grandmother for one year, and then my mother came to
visit, begging me to come back with her, saying that this
time it would be better, and it was. But one night I slept at
my older sister's house, and when I came back home my
mother was completely high and started to beat me, and I
was raped by her boyfriend.

I ran away again to live with my grandmother. While I
was there, I went to Campinas to spend a few days with
my cousin. One night I walked with her to the supermarket
to buy some ingredients to make a cake. She told me to
sit on a bench in a park down the street and wait for her.
It was about ten o'clock. Suddenly two men came by in a
car, pulled me inside, and stopped under a train overpass.
They pulled me out of the car and tried to take my clothes
off. I was able to get away and ran down the street to a taxi
stand where a driver called the police.

From there, the police took me to the government emergency shelter. I could not go back to my cousin's house because she might have been involved in what had happened. They decided I should not go back to my mother's house, either. They had nowhere to send me. . . .

Ileana's story is unique but not exceptional. In northeastern Brazil, in Thailand, in India, and in a thousand other places around our globe, adolescent prostitution plays a major role in regulated and unregulated commerce. Every year in Brazil, 250,000 adolescent and *preadolescent* girls enter the sex trade.[1] And child prostitution is just one face of the problem for those Jesus called "the least of these." Starvation, human slavery, entire people groups in refugee camps, profound generational poverty, imprisonment in subhuman conditions. Not exceptional; it is the normative for millions—perhaps billions—of people.

Take a look at the numbers:

2: Number of children murdered each month *inside* the walls of one children's prison in Brazil.

29: In the time it took you to read the previous page, twenty-nine children died of preventable causes.[2]

1,100,000: More than one million children are locked in prisons, usually in subhuman conditions: block-wall and steel-bar cells with little light or outside air. Their toilet, a hole cut in the concrete in a corner of the cell.[3]

153,000,000: The global economic collapse has pushed the number of social and biological orphans to (conservatively) 153 million. The vast majority of these children are left to survive on their own, without any significant adults in their lives.

200,000,000 and 27,000,000: Two hundred million children are exploited for labor; more than 27 million of the world's people are slaves.[4]

1,100,000,000: If you were to line up all the children in the world side-by-side, every other one of the 2.2 billion children would be malnourished from lack of access to food. That's 1.1 billion (with a *b*) children who do not have sufficient food. More than 800 million people go to bed hungry every day, and 500 million people, more than two times the population of the United States, are on the verge of starvation.

It's hard to get worked up about numbers; when we see figures this big, they become meaningless. But the reality is that every one of these numbers represents a real person. Every one of the 21,000 children who will die of poverty today feels the pangs of hunger as surely as would our child or grandchild, or younger brother or sister. Every child soldier could have been a little boy playing with a toy truck in his front yard. Every girl sold to a man on the streets was someone's innocent daughter.

So what do we do about it?

If we read these numbers through the prism of pity, our first reaction is relief that no one we know is counted among the tragic numbers. Then we may give a few dollars or maybe even take a missions trip to try to make it nominally better for the generic "underprivileged." But the problem is, pity rarely sees the face beyond the number.

A good friend has a framed, embroidered motto on his desk: "*noblesse oblige*" (the obligation of the nobility). I sometimes give him a pretty hard time about it because it can symbolize all that is wrong about the Church's response to issues of poverty and need. It's like an uncomfortable line that was popular in the privileged class of the South in my childhood: "There but for the grace of God go I." Embedded within each phrase can be a subtle (or perhaps not so subtle) classism, elitism, usually with the unspoken undercurrent that we deserve all we have. God has looked on us with favor—and deep down, we know we deserved it.

The condescending pity reflected in these phrases is the very opposite of Christian charity (using that word in the truest sense of 1 Corinthians 13). If you scratch most of us deeply enough, you will probably find a core belief that we somehow have a right to our stations in life. Doing for others is often less an act of grace than it is self-affirmation. By serving the "less fortunate," we confirm the rightness of our privileged status.

At the same time, if we can divorce these phrases from our self-righteousness and condescension, they speak to the very heart of the gospel. There *is* an obligation that comes with having been materially blessed, and it grows from the recognition that the blessing is unmerited. Deeply and profoundly understanding just how blessed we are can be a powerful motivation for blessing others.

That's where love comes into play, and we discover the difference between compassion and pity. Compassion takes a different track than does pity. Compassion is based on the recognition that we are all in this together. It could have worked out differently. What if you had been born in the slums of New Delhi? Would you have obtained your station in life if you had started in a hut in the African bush? What if home was North Korea? Bottom line here: You weren't born into affluence because God loves you more.

Compassion grows out of God-given and God-sanctioned love and demands a lifestyle of engagement, a conscious choice about consumption and generosity, a refusal to see those in need as "other." It means moving beyond our places of comfort and encountering a world that is dirty, ugly, and often painful.

It happened when I was a graduate student in theology and my friend was a senior in college. We were on one of those summer abroad trips that are now ubiquitous but were just then becoming popular. Making our way back from London's West End, I stepped over a drunk or addicted or mentally ill (take your pick) man lying in the subway passage. My friend stopped. "We've got to help."

"No."

"But, we've got to."

"No."

"But . . ."

"No," I said. "Your intervention would not help him anyway. He can go to a shelter; this is not our problem."

And so we walked away, a bit of anger in her eyes; self-certainty in mine. Never my problem, especially when the pain is self-inflicted. I prefer ouchless faith, clean grace.

Compassion.

Interesting word, that *compassion*. It means "to suffer alongside." I don't know how many times someone has said to me, "Your work must be very rewarding," or "This must make you feel really good." It's not, and it doesn't. I remember our first trip to Brazil, hearing the kids' stories, holding the dirty child of the sixteen-year-old prostitute, seeing the boys living under the overpass. My wife, Susan, and I returned home to the question, "Did you have a good time?"

No.

Taking seriously our Lord's command to care for the least of these is not about self-fulfillment or conscience-salving, and certainly not about having a good time. At its essence, it is about suffering alongside those who are hurting. As Paul says in Philippians: "Have this mind among yourselves, which is yours in Christ Jesus, who, though he was in the form of God, did not count equality with God a thing to be grasped, but emptied himself, taking the form of a servant" (Philippians 2:5–7 RSV). Suffering alongside those he came to redeem. Sharing our self-inflicted wounds.

Compassion. It means we don't get to step over those lying in our path.

The Edict

Here's a bit of Bible trivia for you: Only one person in the parables of Jesus is given a name. Do you know who it is? Think about it for a minute.

Lazarus.

Lazarus is a poor beggar who lies at the gate of a rich man's home, hungry, diseased, ignored. The description of Lazarus that Jesus gives in Luke 16 is not very appealing: He was "covered with sores and longing to eat what fell from the rich man's table. Even the dogs came and licked his sores" (vv. 20–21). Recurring theme here: He didn't look like you and me. Not the kind of guy most of us would want to befriend or invite home for dinner. Why don't the heroes in Jesus' stories *look* like heroes?

Interesting turn here. It is not the rich man who has a name, but the poor, crippled beggar. Even more interesting, the name Lazarus means "the one whom God helps."

Did Jesus get the names mixed up? At least at first glance, the rich man is the one God helps and Lazarus is the one God forgot. "There was a rich man who was dressed in purple and fine linen and lived in luxury every day," we're told in verse 19. By virtually any standard, this rich man has found favor with God. Or has he?

The story takes a twist and the tables get reversed. Lazarus dies and the angels carry him to Abraham's side.

Get this picture. In Jesus' day, a formal dinner was held around a low table, and the guests reclined on their left sides, eating with their right hands, essentially leaning against the person on their left—in their bosom, if you will. That means that the guest of honor, the person to the host's right, was resting on the host's side. Now see it? In the Jewish hierarchy, Abraham was heaven's elite of the elite, the patriarch of the Jewish nation. And in this picture, Lazarus was not just some nameless beggar, lying at a rich man's gate; he was the guest of honor at a heavenly feast. Make that *the* heavenly feast.

But the rich man dies and winds up "in Hades, where he was in torment" (Luke 16:23).

Oh. I guess Lazarus *was* the one who God helped.

When we focus on the big picture, this is subversive stuff. You may have the money, the power, and the position now, but that is not how it will work out in the cosmic play. Subversive. Have you heard the old African American spiritual "Rock My Soul in the Bosom of Abraham"? This is where it comes from. The poor slave in the field could sing this song, essentially saying, "I may be the slave now, and you may be the master, but one of these days, one of these days . . ." Do you think the slave owner got it?

Here is a question, though: How does Jesus know the rich man is going to end up in hell? Why is this a foregone conclusion? Obviously God liked him enough to let him be wealthy on earth. He wore all the trappings of blessing. Shouldn't there have been some carry-over? Why hell? Is it just because he is rich? I certainly hope not, because if that's the case, we're all in trouble. If you are wealthy enough to have purchased this book, you are almost certainly among the wealthiest 2 percent of all the people who have ever lived in the world. We are the purple and fine-linen crowd. If wealth condemns to hell, then that's where we are all headed.

The answer has to be something else. Maybe it can be found in some other words of Jesus:

> Then he will say to those on his left, "Depart from me, you who are cursed, into the eternal fire prepared for the devil and his angels. For I was hungry and you gave me nothing to eat, I was thirsty and you gave me nothing to drink, I was a stranger and you did not invite me in, I needed clothes and you did not clothe me, I was sick and in prison and you did not look after me." They also will answer, "Lord, when did we see you hungry or

thirsty or a stranger or needing clothes or sick or in prison, and did not help you?" He will reply, "Truly I tell you, whatever you did not do for one of the least of these, you did not do for me."

Matthew 25:41–45

The least of these. The Lazaruses of the world. Maybe the kid under the overpass. Or the man in the subway. Peripheral people. Tertiary lives.

You did not do for me. Tough words.

I have a friend who relates the story of a Sunday school class he was teaching. On one Sunday they studied a particularly difficult passage. A businessman in the class reflected for a moment on the Scripture and then said, "I bet Jesus wished he hadn't said that."

I don't know about your theology, but my understanding of Scripture is that it is a lot more likely that Jesus meant to say exactly what he said in this passage, and if we wish he had not said these words, it's our problem, not his. There are times in God's Word when we're demanded to call on a faith that pushes us to step beyond our level of comfort and encounter a world that is not always pretty, not always easy, not always nice.

Dirty faith, if you will.

Jesus certainly seems to be pretty serious about it. He doesn't toss around words like *depart, cursed,* and *eternal fire* for effect. He's not given to hyperbole. Hear what he has to say: It is not just our attitude, but also our action toward the least of these that is the standard of what he deems to be righteous or unrighteous. If we understand righteousness to be the product of God's grace, then what Jesus is telling us here is that it is very easy to determine who has experienced the grace of God that transforms the unrighteous into the righteous. You can always identify the righteous by their attitude and activity toward the least of these.

Always.

It is not an indicator, it is not a sign, there is no gray area here. It is a determinant. According to Jesus, if you have experienced God's grace, this is how you will live in relationship to those in need. So it is easy to know where the rich man winds up. He knew Lazarus—he called him by name—but he really couldn't be bothered to care about him, "to do unto him." So that's where James gets it: "Suppose a brother or a sister is without clothes and daily food. If one of you says to them, 'Go in peace; keep warm and well fed,' but does nothing about their physical needs, what good is it? In the same way, faith by itself, if it is not accompanied by action, is dead" (James 2:15–17).

A question: Do we take Jesus seriously today? When the least of these are hoping to pick up the crumbs that fall from the Church's table, I wonder what kind of gospel we are preaching. Let me say this as clearly as I can: The gospel of Jesus Christ cannot be separated from caring for the widow, the orphan, the hungry, the sick, the prisoner.

John says it a bit differently: "But if anyone obeys his word, love for God is truly made complete in them. This is how we know we are in him: Whoever claims to live in him must live as Jesus did" (1 John 2:5–6).

Must live as Jesus did. That's a tough one—one I'm not sure I have completely worked out. But I do know it starts with relationships, both with God and with others—and not just those who look like us. John's point is that we cannot claim that our walk with God is where it should be, or perhaps even that we have a walk with him at all, if every other part of our life doesn't reflect that relationship. Preaching the good news of eternal life while ignoring present pain is an emaciated and impoverished gospel. True righteousness means that we feed, we heal, we touch.

Dirty faith.

It's the kind of faith that cannot be practiced in isolation. To truly love the orphan, the child prostitute, the widow, and the prisoner requires relationships, and perhaps this relationship aspect is what we have lost as a Church. Far too often we want to hire someone to do our Christianity for us, to pay the pastors and missionaries—the "professional" Christians—to do the work we are all called to do. Our financial gifts are the salve for our consciences that tell us we are really being faithful to our Lord's commands. We live in comfortable homes and rarely encounter the lives of the least of these. We are practitioners of a sanitized faith.

Is that the way God designed his work? I remember a line in one of my Christology texts from seminary. The author is long gone from my memory, but his words stay with me: "Wasn't it just like God to become man?"

Yeah, it was.

Because even for God, coming face-to-face with the reality of our humanity—struggling alongside us, feeling the pain we feel, feeling need—was absolutely essential to the gift of himself. How much more true must this be for us?

Living as Jesus did demands relationship with those we are called to serve. Isolation, even if we write big checks to support a ministry, cannot be an option for us. True biblical Christianity means that we get down—in the dirt, if necessary; that we experience life as they experience it; that we view the world from their perspective. *How does it feel when the world steps over you, when the only eye contact you make with the drive-by people is when they are trying to pick you up?* The New Testament knows nothing of an arm's-length Christianity.

Truth be known, my experience is that those who have met the child of the streets face-to-face, those who have hugged the orphan in the slum, those who have looked into hungry eyes, those who have held the child of the prostitute become far more generous. I know it impacted me that way; tithing simply wasn't enough anymore. But true Christian charity—in

33

the 1 Corinthians 13 usage—begins not with our pocketbooks, but with our hearts. Bottom line: You cannot be intimate with God and distant from those he loves.

It's My Problem

Erin is in the back of the car sobbing; it is her first encounter with true poverty.

"Just give me a minute and then I can talk." A few minutes before, she had been sitting on a ragged bed while a little girl and a little boy climbed over her. The little girl was beautiful by any standards, even in her filth, but the three-year-old boy, naked except for a tattered T-shirt, already had the vacant stare so common in the *favela* (slum). We had walked from the girl's sagging scrap sheet-metal home to the boy's shack a few yards behind. A man sat rocking in a straight-legged wooden chair, obviously high; the mother was nowhere in sight.

But now we were back in the car. Erin knows the odds are against these kids. She knows they will probably run away from home to live on the streets, become involved with gangs, and beg or steal to buy food and drugs. She knows the girl will probably sell her body and the boy will probably end up in jail, and they'll both be lucky to survive five years on the streets.

Getting control of her tears, she asks, "I don't get this. Isn't Brazil one of the wealthiest countries in the world?"

"Yes."

"Isn't there enough money for them to take care of their own? Shouldn't this be their problem and not ours?"

Philip, Hope's CEO, turns to look at her, a bit of a hard edge to his response. "You're absolutely right; there's enough money here to fix the problem. There are incredibly wealthy people in this city who ought to be right here, right now, taking care of these kids." He pauses, then says more gently, "Why don't you get out of the car, go back inside, and tell Franciella and Lucas that we're not going to do anything for them because it's not our problem."

Not *my* problem.

The problem is greater than society's unwillingness to intervene; more often than not, the ones who ought to love the child the most are hurting him or her. For the great majority of the world, *orphaned* does not mean parentless. In fact, about 10 percent of orphans are without either parent; the vast majority of children we call orphans have at least one parent.[5] But they have been abandoned, have run away to escape abuse, or have been removed from their homes because of abuse, exploitation, or neglect.

I don't like these parents—and that is really not strong enough to express how I feel. In the one critical task they have been given in life—TAKE CARE OF YOUR CHILD—they have failed. And more often than not, the reality is more grave than not doing well by their kids; very often, those parents actively choose to hurt their children. We all have a problem when we see this.

And so we have a tailor-made excuse to keep our hands clean: not my problem.

Must live as Jesus did.

Here's the point: There are children all over the world whose lives will not change if we—you and I—do not change them. Kids like Franciella and Lucas won't make it unless we get serious about faithfulness to our commission as Christians. This is not clean faith; this is not easy church. It's unpleasant, it's difficult, but it is absolutely necessary.

Dirty faith means their stories can turn out like Ileana's:

. . . so they brought me to Hope Unlimited. Today I believe in transformation. And I am sure that my mother can change. I have not seen her since I ran away, but

I have forgiven her and ask God every day for her salvation.

Today I have found Jesus and am very happy. I have the chance to study, and I hope to achieve my dream of becoming a nurse so I can come back to help the children here at this place, where I learned to walk with my head held high.

It's beautiful, difficult, transformative.
It's dirty faith.

Clay Vessels and Overflowing Hearts

And now abideth faith, hope, charity, these three; but the greatest of these is charity.

1 Corinthians 13:13 KJV

The King's English can be a challenge, but this is a really good translation of the verse. The King James Version catches the original intent of the word. Charity does not mean a giveaway. Rather, it is activity based on intimacy, on love—a word that captures what the follower must be about.

A good word, but a challenge to activity-oriented people.

I am a fixer. When I see a problem, I don't want to talk about it. I don't want to be empathetic. I want to repair it. On the farms and ranches of west Texas where I spent my youth, that's what men did. We fixed things. A colleague once said I come from the Ready, Fire, Aim School of Management. Do something. Now. In my line of work, being a fixer can be real motivation. I can pop out of bed every morning with the full assurance that a good day's work will save the life of another child. I can go to bed at night knowing I have made the world better.

Pretty powerful stuff—but not very biblical.

God really drove this home to me a few years ago. Despite incredible efforts to save it, we were going to lose a residential shelter—what you would call an orphanage—in Brazil. No one could have worked harder, tried more avenues, done anything more to pull it out of the fire. But we were losing. And closing time was minutes away.

We failed; the fixers couldn't fix this one.

But then God stepped in. What all our efforts couldn't achieve in months, his intervention did in minutes.

But God's intervention was the challenge: When the fixer realizes he is not able to make the repair, that it has never been his work, he has to find a new reason to get up in the morning. It isn't my efforts that keep those kids alive, that give them the promise of a future. This is God's purview; I just get to be along for the ride. So, again, why punch the clock? Why put in the effort? After all, there are easier jobs, and God has this one under control.

First Corinthians 13:13: Charity. Love. The real motivation. The biblical motivation.

The easiest analogy that came to me during that time of questioning was my relationship with my wife, Susan. There has not been a single morning in the last two-plus decades when I have gotten out of bed thinking, *I've got to do everything I can today to save my marriage.* I'm not taking it for granted, but that really is not a concern. At the same time, though, every single day of our marriage, I have wanted to do something to make her life better, easier, more fulfilling. Why, if there's no need for me to save our marriage? Because I am motivated by love. And that is how you act when you love. In the same way, I am not saving children; that's God's job. But I am extremely blessed to be part of their redemption.

And that is charity, in the truest Christian sense of the word.

Doing the Divine

Why does God do it this way, this creating and redeeming thing? If you really think about it, the way God chooses to generate new life or transform life does not make a lot of sense. In fact, it is about the messiest way he could do it—because it requires our involvement.

Back in the beginning—still in the garden but after the fall—the sin of Adam and Eve had corrupted all of creation. That means life was going to end; it would not go on forever without intervention. So God had some choices to make about what he would do now that this perfect world he had created had been corrupted by sin. The way I see it, he could have done one of three things—the first two are the most obvious:

1. Let all creation wind down and end. Basically chalk it up to, "This was a grand experiment, but it did not work." So once Adam and Eve die, all the animals are gone, and the existing plants have lived out their time, life is over.
2. Directly re-create. The world is fallen but worth saving. As each generation ends or nears its end, God creates the next generation anew, so there is a constant regeneration of all living things in the world, a new Adam and Eve, a new garden for every generation, if you will.

From where I sit, either one of these seems to be a logical and easy choice for God. If sin is to be the defining characteristic, perhaps he just lets it go away. Or, if this creation is worth having, God essentially starts all over. But he doesn't do it that way. Instead, he chooses the most unlikely path, the way that really does not make any sense, which, in fact, seems wrapped up in failure from the start. . . .

    3. Let the fallen, the corrupt, the sinful participate in the creation and redemption of life.

I want you to think deeply about this: The most sacred trust God could possibly hand to us is precisely what he gives us—his job, creating and redeeming life.

Creation first: He says to us, *I am not doing this anymore; I am not going to bring forth life out of the dust of the earth. This is now your job. I will be alongside you for it, but it's your job.* And so we become responsible for generating new life through sexual creation. The "be fruitful and multiply" thing? God really meant it, and he placed this creation of new life at the very core of our existence.

But—important, really important—the creation of new life is always to occur within the context of a covenant relationship—marriage—and to be an act of love. As the creator of love, God commissions us to create new life and makes it integral to our identity. But then he intimately involves himself in the act of creation, making it a product of love that has its genesis in his heart. So yes, it is our job, but it should never be divorced from his presence.

After that, it gets really interesting: redemption. God most certainly did not have to do it the way he does. Direct engagement with those he redeems would have been much cleaner, much easier. In fact, there are plenty of occasions when God did precisely that. He spoke directly to Abraham, and through the medium of the burning bush to Moses, and even in the New Testament, he directly confronted Saul on the road to Damascus.

But those are the aberrations. For the most part, that is not how God goes about encountering those he will redeem. Jesus' words are the template: "But you will receive power when the Holy Spirit comes on you; and you will be my witnesses in Jerusalem, and in all Judea and Samaria, and to the ends of the earth" (Acts 1:8). For two thousand years now, the ministry of Christ has been through the hands of his people.

Have you ever thought about how radical this is? The Damascus Road experience could have been the norm, not the exception. If God wants to redeem the fallen, the obvious way is for him to directly encounter those to be redeemed. Blind them with a light from heaven, identify himself, and give them the choice. It's quick, it's clean, and it does not have to go through the messy medium of humans.

But that is not the way he almost always chooses to do it. Instead, he entrusts *us* with the gift of his divine love. When it gets delivered, it gets delivered through *us*. Paul really hits it on this one: "For God, who said, 'Light shall shine out of darkness,' is the One who has shone in our hearts to give the Light of the knowledge of the glory of God in the face of Christ. But we have this treasure in earthen vessels, so that the surpassing greatness of the power will be of God and not from ourselves" (2 Corinthians 4:6–7 NASB).

You see the picture? God has this incredible, incredible gift that he wants to share with all his creation. He takes this gift and places it in the most fragile, most unlikely vessel—gift box, if you will—the human heart. The gift is so extraordinary that the fragile vessel can't contain it, and it overflows to redeem all it touches. *You anoint my head with oil; my cup overflows,* and it washes over everyone around it.

41

Perhaps, just perhaps, redeeming others is part of our own redemption.

If we truly were created in the image of God, then the new creation should be a full participant in the gift of the divine. So maybe it does make sense this way; doing the work of God is precisely what the redeemed should be expected to do.

But that redemption work is not solely focused on the eternal picture. Perhaps it is a big picture–little picture thing: The big picture—eternity—is always going to be fuzzy unless the little picture—today—is in focus. I do not find a single incident in the New Testament, with the possible exception of the thief on the cross, where Jesus attended to the eternal needs of a person while ignoring their physical state. He was constantly *Messiah*—deliverer—over both the temporal and the eternal.

Perhaps we miss the idea of the justice of God. We want to balance it against God's love, or, at the very least, make it the flip side of that coin, usually in a sermon about hell. But a biblical understanding of the love of God is actually identical to understanding a just God. God wants a just world—and we are to be the agents of that justice. We are the ones he has entrusted, not just with the message of his eternal grace but with the ability to make *the* difference for the widow, the orphan, the hungry, the sick, the prisoner, the prostitute—today. As far as the world is concerned, we *are* justice.

Look at the words of God through the pen of the prophet Isaiah:

> Is not this the kind of fasting I have chosen:
> to loose the chains of injustice and untie the cords of
> the yoke, to set the oppressed free and break every
> yoke?
> Is it not to share your food with the hungry and to pro-
> vide the poor wanderer with shelter—
> when you see the naked, to clothe them, and not to turn
> away from your own flesh and blood?

42

And then watch what happens in the next verse:

> Then your light will break forth like the dawn,
> and your healing will quickly appear.
>
> Isaiah 58:6–8

In other words, the grace of God breaks out in us at that very moment when we are in the middle of doing this justice thing. We are redeemed, even as we redeem.

Here is the secret of all this: A true focus on the big picture is explicitly what keeps the little picture from becoming fuzzy, not the other way around. And a sure sign that the big picture is out of focus is when the little picture is not clear. Jesus could not ignore the temporal needs of people precisely because he was so in tune with their eternal needs. As C. S. Lewis says, "If you read history you will find that the Christians who did the most for the present world were just those who thought the most of the next. . . . It is since Christians have largely ceased to think of the other world that they have become so ineffective in this."[1]

This is the concept: Out of intimacy with God our hearts are filled to the point of overflowing, and that gush of God's love overwhelms every need we encounter. We become the hands and feet to do what Christ did when he walked this earth. We heal, we fill, we are the salve for a hurting world.

So why is the world hurting . . . and so many of the redeemed are sitting on the sidelines?

Far too often as Christians we set up this distinction between having our cup filled to overflowing and having that excess spill onto others. One of the most beautiful scenes in all of Scripture is the prayer of Jesus in the garden of Gethsemane, just hours before his crucifixion. Mark recounts Jesus' prayer this way: "Abba, Father, for you all things are possible; remove this cup from me; yet, not what I want, but what you want" (Mark 14:36

43

NRSV). The word Jesus uses for *Father* here is intensely personal, much more like "Daddy" than the formal "Father." It reflects the depth of relationship between father and son. But here is the key to understanding this prayer: calling God "Daddy" also meant saying, "Not what I will, but what you will." We do not have the relationship without also having the submission.

The same Jesus who said, "I came that they may have life, and have it abundantly" (John 10:10 NRSV), is also the one who said, "Whoever wants to be my disciple must deny themselves and take up their cross daily and follow me" (Luke 9:23). The abundant life part? We get it. Take up your cross? Not so much. Why do we see the privilege side of faith applying to all of us, but the sacrifice—the giving of ourselves—as reserved for a special few believers, perhaps those with the servanthood gene?

Sometimes our churches lapse into a mercenary Christianity, looking to professional Christians to do this vessel business for us. *We'll write the checks, but we're not getting dirty.* I'll keep beating this drum: New Testament faith cannot be practiced in private. Either the faith will destroy the isolation, or the isolation will destroy the faith. Intimacy with God means relationships with others.

Do you see a gradation of Christians, ranking them to the level of their calling and importance to the kingdom? There are the "super-Christians," who are called to be salt, to be light, and to live out the Beatitudes. They are not just the world changers—the Mother Teresa–level people caring for lepers—but sometimes even the ones in the neighborhood who carry food to the sick or serve as foster parents. Doesn't this commission from Jesus apply to them, not to the rest of us? We are the average Christians: church once or twice a week, not quite tithing but making a run at it, serving on the occasional committee, and perhaps even digging really deep in the pocket for the Christmas or Easter offering. But nothing really hands-on.

important, they are not aimed at two classes of Christians—the super-followers and the rest of us. The ones he called to take up a cross are the same ones to whom he promised abundant life. Even David said, "I will see the goodness of the Lord in the land of the living" (Psalm 27:13).

Are we supposed to take these words seriously?

The big picture part is actually the easy part. I can trust God for my eternity, because it is not right now. It's vague, it's out there. Today may be a different matter. It is a little like retirement planning: I'll trust the experts to take care of my 401(k), but I want control of my wallet because I know what is best for me today.

And I get the "laying up treasures in heaven" part. But what about *my* today? Where does the "live abundantly" part come in? Can I really trust God to make today, this lifetime, not just okay but really, really good?

Charity. There's that word again. The love that overflows and engulfs everything in its path. I know that in my most personal relationships—with my wife, for example—it would be absolutely impossible for my life to be fulfilling if I ignored her needs, if I chose not to make her life better when I have the ability to do so. In the same way, an abundant life, a happy life, a fulfilled life is one that lives out the love of God toward the least of these.

I can say without any reservation that the happiest, most content people I know are those who have taken seriously our Lord's command to minister to the least of these. And I know that people who take that step never look back in regret. But that first step of trusting Jesus is the challenge. *You can manage my eternal 401(k), but I want control of my pocketbook.*

Or perhaps I could learn to trust that he really does love me and wants the best for me.

Trust. It's the beginning of dirty faith.

3

Seeking Relevance in a Post-Christian World

Believers or followers?

There is an apocryphal story, almost certainly not factual, but a good story nonetheless. Let's call it a parable. In the thirteenth century, Pope Innocent IV is in the papal coffers surveying the vast collection of coinage in the church's treasury. St. Thomas Aquinas, out for an afternoon stroll, stops by for a visit. Standing amidst all the wealth, Innocent calls out, "Ah, Thomas, no longer can we say, 'Silver and gold have I none.'" Thomas replies, "But neither can we say, 'In the name of Jesus, rise up and walk.'"

Painful Truths

The case can be made that the modern church, especially in its American manifestation, exists primarily to provide employment to professional Christians.

Now that I have your attention, let's talk.

Before we go too far, a bit of context. I love the Church—and its local manifestation, too. If you are a follower of Christ, love for his bride has to be a foregone conclusion. Paul describes Christ's love for the Church this way: "Christ loved the church and gave himself up for her" (Ephesians 5:25). Conformity to the image of Christ means that we have passion for the Church and its work in the world. It truly is *the* vessel of transformation for a world that has not encountered a loving Father.

But I have to be honest—I am concerned. Really concerned.

I live in a small southern Appalachian town, population around eight thousand. We have about forty-five churches. That's one church for every 177.7 citizens. If, on average, the churches have three staff members, we have one minister for every sixty or so folks in town. And, at the very least, $30 million is invested in our town's church facilities.

Why?

Of course, there are some real doctrinal issues that separate some of us, but there are over thirty Southern Baptist churches in the town and nearby area. I have been in enough of these churches to know that it is the rare church in our city that is even half-filled to capacity.

Really?

I recently had a conversation with a young seminary graduate who was moving as a church planter to a small town with religious demographics not very different from ours, a typical church-on-every-corner southern town. A church planter? Again, *why?* Why are we investing kingdom money on more and more churches, more and more staff? Here's why: For most of its history, the Church has been more interested in consolidating its power than it has in building its ministry. And those of us in the United States are the foremost practitioners of a Christianity turned inward.

Try looking at this from another angle, perhaps call it the "where your treasure is" axiom.

Two-point-five percent. That's the percentage of income that self-identified American evangelicals give to Christian causes—their churches, mission organizations, Christian colleges. Not 15 percent, not even the biblically mandated 10 percent tithe. Just 2.5 percent. My experience tells me that there are a lot of Christians out there for whom the tithe is just a starting point; their gifts put them well above the 10 percent threshold. Factor them in, and this means, overwhelmingly, we as believers are giving back to God in a 0- to 2-percent range.[1]

Unfortunately, that 2.5 percent is not the really devastating number. This is: 97 percent of that tiny 2.5 percent we give goes primarily to benefit other Christians. This basically means that of every $100 of income earned by American evangelicals, about five cents touches those who have not heard that Jesus loves them. A nickel. *There was a rich man dressed in fine linen . . .*

This is not about hard economic times preventing us from giving. In fact, the opposite is true. Since the Great Depression, income has risen on a fairly consistent curve, with only a few blips along the way. At the same time, however, giving as a function of income has steadily decreased.

Simply put, the more we have, the more we keep. The more we are blessed, the less we choose to bless others. *Noblesse oblige?* Indeed.

Many of us have become practitioners of a sterile faith, hiring professional Christians as the mercenaries of the kingdom. There are churches with no greater relevance than the local school, Rotary Club, United Way, or 4-H club.

This isn't dirty faith. It's sterile, sanitized, keep-the-world-at-arm's-length-so-we-can-enjoy-our-blessings faith, a baptized version of the local Y. *Have we become a Church of believers rather than followers?*

51

There may—*may*—have been a time in our past when it was okay to do church this way. The church of the early- to mid-twentieth century, especially in the American South, was the very center of the community. It served as a moral compass, as the social structure that made sure the community—even the part of the community having no formal contact with the church—was contoured in such a manner that culture itself became a reflection of the values (if not the soul) of the church. We made sure all the neighborhood kids were rounded up for a week of immersion in Bible stories at Vacation Bible school; the ladies of the church were sure to stockpile the dinner table and refrigerator when illness showed up, and Thanksgiving and Christmas charity baskets made certain the less fortunate knew we cared about them. But even then, we really did not have to get our hands very dirty.

The church was the moral center of the community, and we were comfortable with this cultural Christianity. It was self-validating, giving us a sense of our rightness and a place of respect. There was a self-assuredness born of the moral stature the church had in the community.

No more. Welcome to the twenty-first century. The community really does not care what the Church has to say anymore. There are 1,001 other cultural influences that clamor for prominence in shaping society. And guess what? They are getting first billing. The Church is, by large, a rearguard action trying to hold on to something that simply doesn't exist today. We are no longer *the* culture, but we keep acting like we are.

We have fallen victim to a deadly trade-off. In order to gain cultural authority, we surrendered our spiritual authority. Once society no longer recognized our cultural authority, we had nothing on which to fall back. We can't do it that way anymore. So perhaps it is time we get back to being the Church Christ called us to be.

The challenge of changing the world is not about our capability: Spending just $30 billion per year could essentially eliminate global starvation and malnutrition; $12 billion per year could provide education for every child on earth; and an additional $15 billion each year could provide universal access to clean water and sanitation.[2] A lot of money? Not really. If Christians chose to give 10 percent of their income, and churches chose to devote 60 percent of that increased giving to "least of these" needs, there would be $98.4 billion available for changing the context internationally with an additional $32.8 billion for domestic missions.[3] And, by the way, as we meet those needs, we also gain the moral and spiritual stature to share with the world the good news that Jesus loves them and died to bring them eternal life.

The question is, do we have the will—or even the interest—to change the context? Maybe not. When asked, "What would you do with an unexpected financial windfall?" 31 percent of Protestant pastors said they would build, expand, or update their church buildings and facilities. Only 7 percent said they would give more to foreign missions and evangelism.[4]

Do you know that the average American church spends around $330,000 for every conversion?[5] And that is defining *conversion* very loosely, including the children of church families who become church members. Three hundred and thirty thousand dollars! What could a church in Mozambique do for its AIDS-stricken community with that same $330,000? Or how many sex-trafficked girls in Thailand could be given the hope of a future where they do not sell their bodies? Or how many children in a Mexican village could learn to read, master a vocation, and also learn that Christ died for them with what it takes to secure one conversion in the U.S.? Does God value American souls so much more?

Now, I am not naïve. I understand that throwing money at problems doesn't always solve them. At the same time, excusing

53

our greed by saying "money won't fix it" is a canard. That is too easy, a "not my problem" escape. And for the U.S. church to sit on its hands when there is so much need is an absolute abdication of our moral and spiritual obligation.

We have spent two thousand years building a hierarchy that is internally focused; why don't we spend the next two thousand years looking beyond our walls?

It's time for a revolution. We need to take the needs of the world around us seriously. The Church needs to be reminded that spending 85 percent of its resources on salaries, facilities, and other internal needs of the congregation makes a mockery of the Great Commission. In 1890 Frederic Huntington wrote, "It is not scientific doubt, not atheism, not pantheism, not agnosticism that in our day and in this land is likely to quench the light of the gospel. It is proud, sensuous, selfish, luxurious, church-going, hollow-hearted prosperity." It seems nothing's changed. Where is the dirty faith, the compassion?

To be fair, there are some churches out there that have figured out this thing. You can recognize them the moment you encounter them. They really are doing church, New-Testament-re-creating-the-ministry-of-Christ-constantly-and-consistently church. But I am afraid they are the exception rather than the rule.

To a more important question: Where is God in all this? How has spiritual narcissism impacted the activity of God in our churches? Can we claim his power, his equipping, his presence when we are not acting as his people? Look at Acts: "But you will receive power when the Holy Spirit comes on you," but it does not stop there: "and you will be my witnesses" (1:8). Jesus' words and intent are clear here. *You are going to be blessed with a divine empowerment, but that empowerment comes with an expectation of use; you are going to re-create the ministry I had when I walked this earth.* One does not happen without the other. Receiving the power absolutely means you must be the witnesses.

Did you ever break an arm or a leg and have it completely immobilized in a cast? Remember what you saw when the cast came off? Muscle gone. No definition, no tight skin, just limp, pretty much useless flesh, and certainly no power. Atrophy is the result of not using muscles, and it applies to the spiritual body as well as the physical. If we are not witnesses, we don't have power.

I grew up in a go-to-church-every-time-the-doors-were-open family. Sunday morning, Sunday night, Wednesday night—did not matter, we were there. And for the most part I was okay with that. Church was completely integrated into our lives. That is where my friends were, and church was what we did. But there was one Sunday of the year I always tried to avoid: Missions Sunday. I did not want to be there. Absolutely hated it. And the reason was really pretty simple. I thought all missionaries were liars. They would stand behind the pulpit and tell one lie after another about the things they had seen God do. And I did not believe them, because God doesn't act like that. Not anymore. Maybe he did two thousand years ago, but he doesn't today. So I sat at the back of the church, rolling my eyes at one more story I knew did not happen the way it was being told.

But then I traveled to a remote Mexican village, and I faced evil in a Brazilian slum. I met children locked in bleak prison cells. I held the child of a prostitute. And I saw God do things he just doesn't seem to do here anymore.

Maybe we have outgrown God and don't really need him anymore. New concept here: the self-sufficient Church. There is actually a teaching of Jesus that talks about this. Well, not precisely this, but the point should be well-taken. Matthew relates the story of a rich man who comes to Jesus asking him the secret of eternal life. Jesus gives him the easy part first: keep the commandments—no adultery, no stealing, no lying, honor your parents, and love your neighbors. The rich man replies that he has that covered; what else does he have to do?

This is the tough part. Jesus answers him, "If you want to be perfect, go, sell your possessions and give to the poor, and you will have treasure in heaven. Then come, follow me" (Matthew 19:21). Too tough. The rich man walks.

Jesus then turns to his followers for some follow-up discipleship: "Truly I tell you, it is hard for someone who is rich to enter the kingdom of heaven." And then, "Again I tell you, it is easier for a camel to go through the eye of a needle than for someone who is rich to enter the kingdom of God" (Matthew 19:23–24). Did you catch the subtle but important switch in wording? I think Jesus is making a distinction here between the kingdom of heaven and the kingdom of God. The kingdom of heaven is a place, a destination, if you will. It is the ultimate home of the redeemed. It is difficult, very difficult, for a rich man to get there, because doing the faith and grace thing can be a challenge with a full wallet. But the kingdom of God is a state of being, a way of existence, and it borders on the impossible for a rich person to get *there*, because, you see, the kingdom of God is not some remote, future promise. It is to be realized here, now. It is a state of living in total dependence upon God, of finding everything we need in him. The rich man really doesn't need God—can make it fine without him. So entering that state of dependence is virtually impossible—as difficult as a camel passing through the eye of a needle.

And in today's reading of the parable, the Church has become the rich man. Try reading it this way: *Again I tell you, it is easier for a camel to go through the eye of a needle than for a church that is rich to enter the kingdom of God. "No longer can we say, 'Silver and gold have I none.'" "But neither can we say, 'In the name of Jesus, rise up and walk.'* " We've pretty much outgrown this God-dependence stuff. We can take care of ourselves. No kingdom of God for us.

The good news is, Jesus doesn't leave it hanging there. "With man this is impossible, but with God all things are possible" (Matthew 19:26). In fact, the very next day, Luke records that Zacchaeus, a rich, conniving, thieving tax collector, comes to faith in Jesus, but even then, "Zacchaeus stood up and said to the Lord, 'Look, Lord! Here and now I give half of my possessions to the poor, and if I have cheated anybody out of anything, I will pay back four times the amount' " (Luke 19:8).

Atrophied muscles can be rehabbed.

So let's talk about becoming relevant again, and perhaps finding the kingdom of God again. To kick that off, a story: Philip and I are sitting in his small office in Campinas, Brazil, talking about a new project we need to start. A woman who works in the office hears our conversation stall and walks in and hands him a letter addressed to *Tio Philippe*—Uncle Philip. It is from one of the older girls at the City of Youth. Philip begins to read aloud, translating to English from the Portuguese for me as he goes:

> Dear Uncle Philip:
>
> In our Bible study we have been talking about intimacy with God. This is what I want for my life, so each day I pray, "God, show me your face." But God doesn't show me his face. So I pray again, "Please, God, show me your face." But I hear nothing from God. So I cry out to him, "Why will you not show me your face?" And God answered me. He said, "But Carolena, I show you my face every day. You are not hungry today. You go to a good school. You have a family who loves you. You have a safe place to sleep."

And I realized that everywhere God said he was showing me his face was a place that you have made for me.
So, Uncle Philip, for me, you are the face of God.

Love, Carolena

That's it, right there. That is relevance. That is what it looks
like, that is what it sounds like. I may not always be able to
describe it, but I know it when I see it.

It all begins with an understanding of what Church is. Church
is not what we do on Sunday that then gives birth to mission.
In fact, just the opposite is true. Church doesn't create mission;
mission creates Church. Virtually every church today has a missions committee or a missions program or a missions pastor. The
summer youth missions trip is a highlight of the church calendar.
(Isn't it amazing how much need there is in Orlando?) And "doing
missions" is one of the compartments that defines a church.

But this is wrong. Very wrong. Because what the Church *is*
is missions. Missions is not the end of Church; it is the genesis.
When the Church looks in the mirror, it should see missions.
Missions is not one of the things that the Church does, on a
level playing field with worship, discipleship, stewardship, etc.,
and it is certainly not something we do from our excess. The
Church *is* missions.

Let's approach it this way. From a New Testament perspective, the Church is the body of Christ. That means, as far as the
world is concerned, they see Christ by seeing us. *For me, Uncle
Philip, you are the face of God.* Whatever Christ was about in
the world is what we are to be about in the world. And for the
early Church, the one dominant understanding of Christ was
that he was Messiah. By definition, he was the one who would
deliver, the one who would save. And the Church is a messianic
community. Through the power of the Holy Spirit, we are the
ones who bring deliverance, who bring salvation.

Never, never in the New Testament is the spiritual authority divorced from the physical reality. The two are inseparable. Look at Luke's recounting of the healing of the paralytic. You remember the story. Jesus is teaching, and Pharisees and teachers of the law are sitting there. The friends of a paralyzed man try to bring him in the front door, but the crowds are too thick, so they take him to the roof, remove some tiles, and lower the paralyzed man down in front of Jesus. Really serious friends here. Jesus looks at the man lying at his feet, and, in my version of the story, glances up with a grin at the friends peering down through the hole in the roof. *This will get their attention.* "Friend, your sins are forgiven." Don't you know the Pharisees came out of their seats on that one? "Who is this fellow who speaks blasphemy? Who can forgive sins but God alone?"

Jesus gets it, understands the quandary. "Which is easier: to say, 'Your sins are forgiven,' or to say, 'Get up and walk'? But I want you to know that the Son of Man has authority on earth to forgive sins." Then comes the most important "so" you will ever hear: "So he said to the paralyzed man, 'I tell you, get up, take your mat and go home'" (Luke 5:20–24).

Do you see it? How did Jesus establish his spiritual authority? By demonstrating his material authority. The power to change an eternity—and a today—are precisely the same.

But we do need to give some credit here. The Pharisees do ask the right question, even if it is rhetorical: "Who can forgive sins but God alone?" And the answer resonates for us today, now. *God alone.* And the God who forgives sin is the God who heals.

That is the important part to this. God, alone. Jesus' authority came from beyond himself. Its locus was in his relationship with the Father. Earlier in chapter 5, Luke records, ". . . the news about him spread all the more, so that crowds of people came to hear him and to be healed of their sicknesses. But Jesus often withdrew to lonely places and prayed" (Luke 5:15–16).

More than the ability to resurrect the dead and heal the blind and handicapped—what fascinates me most in Jesus is his dependence on God as Father. A Father who has preference for the worst men and women of this world. A Father who loves those who don't deserve to be loved and chooses the ones who do not deserve to be chosen. A Father who is not focused on a sinner's past, but one who embraces the promise of hope in every abandoned child, broken man, hurting woman. And what we see in the life of Jesus is the constant reflection of his Father's identity.

The trajectory is like this: Out of an intimacy with and dependence on God grows a heart for those He loves. If the Church is self-focused and ineffectual, it is because a lack of intimacy with God shapes our identity. This is where we start, in personal and corporate relationship with God who loves us and wants to be deeply, deeply connected to the very core of our being. And out of that intimacy will grow a love for those Christ loves.

I want you to envision a different kind of Church with me. Think about this for a moment: How much more do we talk in our churches today about believing rather than following? In my experience, the vast majority of churches are focused on proclamation, and the product of proclamation is belief. To no small degree, we are a Church of believers in Christ rather than a community of followers of Christ. We are much more concerned with orthodoxy (making sure we believe the right things, which leads to the church-on-every-corner syndrome) than we are with orthopraxy (making sure we practice the right things—living out the commandments to love God and love our neighbors).

But that is not biblical. In the New Testament, belief is never an end to itself. Without exception, belief is always a precursor, setting the table for following. Look what James has to say about it: "You believe that there is one God. Good! Even the demons believe that—and shudder. You foolish person, do you want evidence that faith without deeds is useless?" (James 2:19–20). The ministry of Christ and the re-creation of that ministry in the Acts of the apostles never took proclamation and theological discourse out of the context of caring for the needs of society's outcasts. In fact, in the early Church, whenever doctrine became the centerpiece (see 1 Corinthians), the Church fell into disarray. The Church thrived when its focus was service. *And God daily added to their number.*

I don't want to get off track here. Doctrine *is* important, but always within the context of the acting Church. Never theology for theology's sake.

So what does a local church that lives this out look like? First, it is a church where intimacy with God is obvious. This is another one of those "I know it when I see it" kind of things. You know the married couple in the neighborhood who is just so obviously in love with each other? Nothing you can really put a finger on, but everyone knows it. The looks, the smiles, the holding hands when they are way past forty. The obvious preference for each other's company. The in-syncness. Nothing definitive, but the whole packet makes it clear: These folks are crazy in love.

It's the same way with a church that is intimate with God. It is a church that regularly spends time in his presence, where there is an obvious affection for the relationship. It is a church where his priorities, his values are the center.

I have been reading the Psalms a lot of late. There is a constantly recurring theme in the psalms of David: seeking the face of God. "My heart says of you, 'Seek his face!' Your face, Lord, I will seek" (Psalm 27:8). This was a consuming passion for David. But quite honestly, it is not a concept that is immediately easy to grasp. What does it mean to seek the face of

God? Let's try it this way. Remember when you were a teenager and you had that first crush—that really serious fifteen-year-old's "I'm in love for the rest of my life" crush? And being in the presence of the one you loved was just the most important thing in the world? That's David here. "One thing I ask from the Lord, this only do I seek: that I may dwell in the house of the Lord all the days of my life, to gaze on the beauty of the Lord and to seek him in his temple" (Psalm 27:4). He is like a teenage boy with a first crush. He has a passion—a love for God—that is all-consuming.

And that's what it has to be for the church. It becomes a place where love for God and the seeking of his face is an all-consuming passion.

Second, the ministry of the church reflects that passion for God, and his priorities become our priorities. To be crass about it, follow the dollars. Does the church budget reflect making sure the membership is comfortable, fellowshiped, and well cared for, or does it re-create the ministry of Christ to the widow, the orphan, the hungry? Do we tell others that Christ loves them? *But where your heart is . . .* Do we invest in the things that make a kingdom difference, or do we dress our congregations in purple and fine linen? Look also at where the church spends its time and efforts. How central is missions to the church program? Passion for God will always result in obedience. And obedience to God always looks beyond ourselves.

Wait a minute, this sounds almost biblical. "The most important one," answered Jesus, "is this: 'Hear, O Israel: The Lord our God, the Lord is one. Love the Lord your God with all your heart and with all your soul and with all your mind and with all your strength.' The second is this: 'Love your neighbor as yourself.' There is no commandment greater than these" (Mark 12:29–31).

What happens then? Go back to David. His love for God was not unidirectional. The prophet Samuel called him "a man after God's own heart." He loved God, but God also so obviously loved him. In passion and obedience, we become the Church that God loves and blesses.

And then we can say, *"In the name of Jesus, rise up and walk."*

PART TWO

FACES

Love Is the Final Apologetic

Cassidy literally grabbed me by the collar immediately after the service. "I finally understand that verse"—a question in my eyes—"the 'He had no place to lay his head' verse. Tonight, for the first time, I understand it."

We were at Saturday evening worship the night before Palm Sunday at The Net Fellowship, a church formed by former street children who are graduates of Hope Unlimited's residential program. Joining the graduates, their families, and members of the community who have become part of The Net were about 120 children who lived at the Hope campus in Campinas, Brazil. We worshiped with those children and young adults, strains of "Hosanna, you are my King" woven throughout the service as language barriers melted away.

Cassidy, an intense burning apparent in his eyes, continued, "I learn experientially, and here tonight I finally understood those words about Jesus, the 'He had no place to lay his head' verse. He was saying that these are his people. These are the ones he identifies with. These kids didn't have a home, a place to sleep. They are the ones like him. Not us, them.

"These are his people."

want to leak grace. I want to be so overwhelmed by the presence of God that his reality in my life is manifestly evident to everyone with whom I come into contact. I want the grace of God to be the basic fact of my existence.

And what will that look like?

Perhaps, just perhaps, it may well be most evident in the way I respond to those who Scripture calls the fatherless, those we call orphans. The case can be made that our treatment of children—and specifically orphans—is a defining characteristic of what it means to be a follower of God. Look at the language of the Old Testament:

Exodus 22:22–23: "Do not take advantage of the widow or the fatherless. If you do and they cry out to me, I will certainly hear their cry."

Deuteronomy 27:19: "Cursed is anyone who withholds justice from the foreigner, the fatherless or the widow."

Psalm 10:14: "You are the helper of the fatherless."

Isaiah 1:17: "Learn to do right; seek justice. Defend the oppressed. Take up the cause of the fatherless; plead the case of the widow."

Caring for the orphan is not just something we are commanded to do; it is the essence of our identity. We accept because we are accepted. We love without reference to merit because we receive unmerited love. We adopt because we are adopted. Hear this again and again: As we stand before God, there is no qualitative difference between us and the most desperate child of the street. But, far too often, we fundamentally misunderstand who we are.

Have you ever heard the old adage, "He was born on third base and thought he hit a triple"? That's us. Scratch most of us deeply enough and you will find that we really believe we somehow deserve our station in life. *There but for the grace of God go I.*

But that's not biblical.

The imagery of Scripture is always that every one of us is an orphan, estranged from God. First Chronicles 29:15 says, "We are foreigners and strangers in your sight, as were all our ancestors. Our days on earth are like a shadow, without hope." But the story never ends there. The picture of Scripture is that, yes, we are strangers, we are orphans, we are without hope, but God . . .

But God . . .

We'll get back to completing this sentence in a while, but let's first look at this phrase for a bit. How often does the point of stasis in a story turn on the phrase, "But God . . ."?

Susan and I first visited Brazil in the fall of 2007. Our first night there, we joined Philip and a group of girls and their houseparents for a pizza party at a local *rodizio*. The girls were used to American visitors, and all went out of their way to make us feel welcome, some even practicing their very limited English on us. Except one girl. It was obvious she didn't quite fit in. She wanted to communicate, wanted to be like the rest of the girls, but she did not know how. We tried to give her a bit of special attention, eventually learning her name was Graziella, and she was twelve years old.

The next day, trying to get our arms—and minds—around this ministry called Hope Unlimited for Children, Susan and I spent some time with Adriana, a vivacious social worker who had an evident and God-blessed passion for seeing transformation in the lives of street children. Adriana's English was only marginally better than our Portuguese, so Philip mediated our conversation. Curious about the previous night, we asked her to tell us Graziella's story. We learned that the juvenile authorities had brought Graziella to campus only a day or two before. She had never known her father; he was one of the exchangeable boyfriends who lived with her mother, a prostitute in one of the poorer *favelas* in Campinas. When Graziella was eleven, her dying mother was put in a government-run AIDS hospice, and Graziella's sixteen-year-old sister was given her guardianship. The first night, *the first night*, Graziella was raped by her sister's lesbian gang.

Adriana continued speaking, but Philip stopped translating. He was not quite arguing with her, but it was clear he was somewhat incredulous and wanted to get the story right. *Her own sister . . . ?* After a minute or so, he closed his eyes to compose himself, and then began to tell the story again. After that first rape, her sister began selling Graziella on a nightly basis to men or women for group sex.

Her sister.

Horrified, Susan and I looked at Adriana. Tears stained her cheeks. I took a deep breath. "Adriana, what kind of chance does Graziella have? I know in the U.S., a child traumatized that severely would be institutionalized, probably damaged beyond recovery."

Now it was Adriana's turn to be horrified.

We would give up on Graziella?

Adamantly, *"Mas Deus."*

But God . . .

There is a point to this. As horrifying as Graziella's story is, she was in no greater need of the transforming love of God than you and I are. If he is capable of doing it for us, he can transform her.

Back to the Scripture. Paul in Galatians 4 said, "But when the set time had fully come, God sent his Son, born of a woman, born under the law, to redeem those under the law, that we might receive *adoption* to sonship. Because you are his sons, God sent the Spirit of his Son into our hearts, the Spirit who calls out, 'Abba, Father.' So you are no longer a slave, but God's child; and since you are his child, God has made you also an heir" (vv. 4–7).

And we are the hands of her transformation. We care for the Graziellas of this world precisely and specifically because God has adopted us. We have been born again in his image, and as he hears the cry of the orphan, so do we.

As noted earlier, the recent international recession has pushed the number of orphans worldwide to 153 million, some saying as high as 167 million. Every country, every corner of the world. It is the reality of existence for somewhere around one out of every fifteen children. Many are biological orphans; some are social orphans. In a place like Mozambique, where war, disease, and famine have decimated the population, probably 90 percent of orphans have no living parents, and, very often, no aunt, uncle, cousin, or grandparent to offer a home or shelter. In other places, like Brazil, where there is an unhealthy culture of abandonment and exploitation, as few as 11.3 percent of orphans have no parent. The fact is simply that the homes of their mothers or fathers are not safe or accepting places for them.

But there is no need to distinguish between categories of orphans: Every one of the 153 million children is hurting, lonely, and in desperate need—and we are the answer.

Let the number sink in. *One hundred fifty-three million children*. The United States has a total population of about 300 million; 153 million is everyone west of the Mississippi and a few back on the other side. If it were a country unto itself, the State of Orphans would be the ninth most populous country in the world, larger than Russia or Japan.[1]

Every day, as many as 40,000 more children become orphans or are abandoned by their parents, and 250,000 children are adopted each year. *About as many children become orphans in any one week as are adopted in a year.* Annually, fourteen million children age out of the care systems—that is 38,356 orphans aging out every day, one child every 2.2 seconds.

And what happens to these kids? This is where the implications, not only for the kids but for society, get really frightening. Studies have shown that somewhere around 12 percent of these children will take their own lives before they reach eighteen. Worldwide, girls who have been orphaned are ten times more likely to sell their bodies to survive than girls in stable families; some studies have the percentages of orphaned girls becoming prostitutes as high as 60 percent. As high as 70 percent of orphaned boys will spend time in jail or prison for criminal offenses.

This is serious. The issue, though, is how serious *we* are willing to be. Are we willing to do something about it?

I want to be very honest with you. Some of these kids are cute and cuddly small children, with infectious laughs and bright smiles—poster children for adoption, the kind who will pull the heartstrings the moment you see their pictures. But most are not. Many have been on the streets or sometimes worse, warehoused in state-funded institutions that have compounded the damage to their bodies, minds, hearts, and souls. They suffer the effects of fetal alcohol syndrome; they have reactive attachment disorder; they have the drug habits of the streets. They are thieves, prostitutes, angry at the world.

And they are children. Children God loves as deeply as he loves you or me.

Jesus loves me this I know, for the Bible tells me so. Little ones to him belong; they are weak, but he is strong.

Jesus loves me. Jesus loves them, and he gave himself for them, that they might become sons and daughters of God.

This is the essence of dirty faith.

Leaking Grace

C. H. Spurgeon, the nineteenth-century pastor of the Tabernacle Church in London and one of the greatest English-language preachers of any generation, was also absolutely committed to seeing his church live out the gospel by its care for the fatherless. During his day, public orphanages were little more than warehouses for children (think *Oliver Twist*), and their conditions were appalling. Set against a background of brutal indifference and disdain by society in general, the work of Spurgeon and his fellow clergyman George Müller to develop Christian charity in England was a profound statement about the love God and his people have for every child.

A wonderful story is told that Spurgeon, leaving one of the orphanage houses built by Tabernacle Church, was accosted by one of London's well-known atheists demanding that Spurgeon, on the spot, provide proof of the existence of God. Spurgeon paused, looked back at the home for orphans behind him, and responded by paraphrasing Elijah: "The God that answers by orphanages, let him be Lord."

I wish I could come up with answers like that.

Do you want the ultimate and absolute proof of God's existence? It is not a scientific or rhetorical syllogism that logically constructs evidence of God. It is not a dispassionate argument that will convince the unbiased. The ultimate proof of a loving God is the reproduction in our lives of that same love. Love truly is the final apologetic. If you look at the history of the Church, especially before the twentieth century, our watermark is that we care for orphans in a world where they have never been a priority. *That* is how we know there is a God.

I won't go church historian on you here, but even a cursory glance at our legacy is that we have taken orphan care—with plenty of highs and lows—pretty seriously for the last two thousand years. The Church came into being in a cultural context that did not find any particular value in human life, and certainly not in the lives of infants and children. In Roman society, any infant could be abandoned without legal repercussions or even social stigma for a variety of causes: illegitimacy, deformation, or simply because the family had too many children.

In the growing Christian movement, however, the Church fathers consistently and conspicuously called upon followers of Christ to be faithful to Scripture's demand that we care for the orphan. Virtually every early writing on Christian conduct stressed the importance of caring for children without parents. Eusebius, the Apostolic Constitutions, Lactantius, Ignatius, Polycarp, Justin Martyr . . . the list goes on and on, but every one of them called on the early Church to care for orphans. One writer goes so far as to say that the orphan had only three possibilities in life: death, slavery, or Christian adoption. Did you know that in some places it's still true today?

Orphan care is our identity—and has been for two thousand years.

But there is a mirror side to this, too. If we are not taking care of the orphan, then we are denying the reality of God in our lives—of our own adoption. I cannot begin to tell you how many times someone has said to me something along the lines of, "It is such a wonderful work you are doing, but God just has not called me to that."

Well, actually, yes, he has. Perhaps not to adopt, or even to foster (we'll get into the issue of "calling" and adoption and foster care in a few pages), but he has called you to care for the orphan. Very specifically.

Orphan care is not something we can pick from a smorgasbord of good things any Christian can do. It is not a faith elective. Let me grab an analogy here. We are not welcomed by God to pick and choose among the Ten Commandments: "Today I think I'll work on the 'Have no gods before me' commandment and maybe tomorrow on that adultery prohibition." I don't think that was God's intent. It was all commandments, all followers, all the time.

In the same manner, caring for the fatherless is never depicted in Scripture as an optional activity for the follower of Christ. In the book of James, it becomes *the* definition of the kind of religion we are to practice: "Religion that God our Father accepts as pure and faultless is this: to look after orphans and widows in their distress and to keep oneself from being polluted by the world" (1:27).

See the balance here: Caring for widows and orphans is given every bit as much weight and importance as being pure. Righteousness or personal holiness or godliness or whatever term we want to use to describe normative Christianity is as much a function of how we interact with the orphan as it is personal piety and purity. We like a sanitized faith. Far too often discipleship is seen as between us and God: I have a daily quiet time, I worship, and I live a pure life. Good, that's a piece of the puzzle. But getting dirty, living in relationship with those who are in contextual pain, is absolutely intrinsic to our identity.

So, yes, we are not just called to care for orphans, we are *commanded*. From a solely practical standpoint, this has to be the job of every Christian. As mentioned before, of the fourteen million children who become biological or social orphans this year, only about 250,000 of them will be adopted. There is no place here for any of us to sit on the sideline. Adoption or foster care may not be in your future (again, postponed discussion), but you must be involved. It takes all of us.

But even beyond *their* need, this is what we need to be doing, perhaps what we cannot help but do. The very nature of grace means we cannot keep it to ourselves. The psalmist said, "You anoint my head with oil; my cup overflows" (Psalm 23:5). The biblical picture of God's love for us is never one of private grace; it is a love that reproduces itself.

So What Will the Church Do?

I want to toss out a caveat here. In caring for the fatherless, there are the easy questions, the moderately difficult questions, and there are the tough questions. The easy ones surround the beautiful, no-issue infants moving through the adoption process. There are many, many parents waiting for these kids, and that is as it should be. Please do not hear criticism here, because there is none. Thank you for loving these children as your own. It is, however, simply a stated fact: There will always be homes for these kids because lots of families want them.

Then there are the moderately hard questions. What do we do with kids from international backgrounds, who may or may not be healthy? Kids who clearly have an issue or two? Babies who have been warehoused, and who, even though still infants, will always have trouble forming attachments? One of the real sea changes in recent years is the number of families who have stepped up in faith for these kids, opening their homes even when they know the challenges they will face and the lack of certainty about outcomes.

And then there are the really tough questions. What is our answer for kids far too long in a broken foster care system? International children of the streets? Girls who have been trafficked? Kids damaged by indifferent, inadequate, or even abusive care in orphanages? Boys and girls who, statistically, are not going to make it?

The word to the Church is this: Take care of those easy cases, but, for the love of God, don't abandon the difficult or even the "impossible" cases. Those children did not choose to be who or where they are. And the love that God has for us compels us to love them. I've had the chance to love many of these children over the last several years, and I know that their desire for love, for family, for a future, burns just as brightly as it does in the child living in your neighborhood—or in your home.

So how do we as churches, as the Church, do something about this reality? Of course, absolutely, do the easy stuff. Put Orphan Sunday on the church calendar. Put child rescue programs in the church budget, or better yet, make this kind of mission focus the heart of the church budget. Adopt an existing orphan program. Take your young adults on a mission trip specifically to minister alongside those who work with street kids, who provide shelter for the homeless child, who give the teenage prostitute an alternative. Do this. Now.

But do the hard stuff, the very hard stuff, too. In fact, let's talk about that. How does a church get really serious about caring for the fatherless? The key is intentionality. Can you imagine a church today that does not have some type of intentional and focused outreach/evangelism program, and some type of discipleship program? Not if it still wants to call itself a church. You better take faith reproduction seriously, or you will not be in business long.

But what about orphan care? What does God expect of us? *To look after orphans and widows in their distress and to keep oneself from being polluted by the world.* Evangelism? Absolutely. Discipleship? That's our DNA. Orphan care? Not so much.

Why not, if this is what Christ has called us—adopted us—to do? Perhaps it is because it takes a different type of commitment

77

to care for orphans than it does to do discipleship or evangelism. Whether we should or not, we generally can compartmentalize those two pieces of our lives. Evangelism, maybe, if the right situation arises and the "evangelee" brings it up. Discipleship, sure. Sunday school, perhaps a midweek small group, and, if we are really serious, a daily time of Bible study and prayer. I am not saying this is the way it should be, but for most of us, even the very committed, our faith fits comfortably within the context of day-to-day living.

It doesn't interrupt who we are.

But this orphan thing is not quite as simple. A child does not need care and attention only on Sunday mornings. She doesn't get hungry just once a day. You cannot love her only when it's convenient. It is an all-consuming reality. Too much to ask?

And now for that twice-postponed discussion. I keep handing us all an out: Perhaps God hasn't called you to foster or orphan care. Pretty much a perspective with a built-in escape hatch for any of us, and generally my perspective. But then I met Bishop W. C. Martin and his congregation in a small church in Possum Trot, Texas.[2] Eighty-eight families in the little church. *Seventy-two foster and adopted children.* And then I heard the story of Calvary Chapel in Ft. Lauderdale, Florida, and the two hundred kids who are now in long-term foster care within the church community, and the thirty to forty kids adopted by church members there *every year.*[3]

Perhaps it is less a matter of calling than it is of hearing.

Maybe we are all called, and perhaps it could be that our lack of being called is actually a function of being tone deaf to the voice of our Lord. *Lord, when did we see you hungry or thirsty or as a stranger or needing clothes or sick or in prison, and did not help you?* How often is spiritual insensitivity the root of disobedience?

But we're not called. . . .

78

And since we're not, most of the 153 million kids without families know hunger, loneliness, and despair as their all-consuming reality.

Let me suggest to you that the Church does have the answer, but it takes a different way of looking at the problem, and a very different way of being Church—or at least very different from the way we are doing it now. From Acts 2: "All the believers were together and had everything in common. They sold property and possessions to give to anyone who had need" (vv. 44–45). That's it. That's the model. But let's make sure we understand it.

I do not think the intent here is promotion of communal living or that every one of us should turn over everything we have to the Church. That is not the point here. The message of the early Church is simple and consistent: "We are all in this thing together." In the New Testament, just as there is no private discipleship, neither is there self-sufficient Christianity. Galatians 6:2 tells us, "Carry each other's burdens, and in this way you will fulfill the law of Christ." You do not get to hold it to yourself, but neither do you have to carry it by yourself.

Would more families be ready to open their homes to the orphan if we started really acting like the Church? Here's a "what if" picture: a Sunday school class at a suburban church. Fifteen families or so, and they decide to get serious about caring for orphans. But the idea of fostering or adopting is just too overwhelming for any of the couples in the class. But (do we need a *Mas Deus* here?) what if the class members decided to really immerse themselves in care and provision for each other, as the Church did in Acts 2? What if one family were to take the lead, be the foster or adoptive family of record, but multiple couples commit to be this child's family? Someone takes after-school tutoring several days a week. Someone else takes care of a lawn because the parents' time has suddenly gotten short. Families in the class provide two meals every week, from now on, to share the task of providing a home for a couple of children. Perhaps the task isn't insurmountable after all. *We're in this thing together.* What if "all the believers were together and had everything in common"?

A bridge too far? Nope. Some churches are actually taking the orphan problem seriously, carrying each other's burdens, and changing the lives of the fatherless. But we'll hold off talking about them for a few chapters. Unfortunately, though, getting really serious about orphans seems to be the province of a few churches rather than an identifier of *the* Church.

Five hundred years after Luther and the original, you want a new Reformation of the Church? This is it.

Or perhaps your small church adopts an orphanage that provides the only home that sex-trafficked kids have ever known. Wait, this isn't an escape hatch. I am talking serious, dirty faith kind of adoption. A we-are-going-to-have-to-change-our-lifestyle level of involvement. A rewrite-the-church-budget (and probably a few family budgets, too) immersion in changing the lives of some hopeless kids. *All the believers were together and had everything in common.* What if these kids are a part of your church family, too, even if they live on another continent?

Here is the point: What we are doing now is not working. Kids are bouncing through the foster care system and families every day. We hear stories of kids permanently assigned to foster care who go through three, six, thirty different families before aging out of the system. One hundred fifty-three million children are without homes, but our Sunday school class has new carpet and we're growing spiritually.

Perhaps this time it needs to be a Revolution rather than a Reformation.

The bottom line is this: Our God is in the transformation business, and we are to be right there in it with him.

Mas Deus. Remember Graziella, the twelve-year-old Susan and I thought would be damaged beyond salvage? About sixteen months after that initial encounter, I was standing at the back of the City of Youth chapel during a Saturday evening worship service. As the service drew to a close, Pastor Derli invited everyone accepting the transforming love of Christ for the first time to stand. Very low-key, no high-pressure evangelism. First one, then another, and then, finally, eight or ten children standing. Pastor Derli asked that a friend and a staff member go stand and pray with each child. Friends stood and embraced friends; members of Hope's staff wrapped loving, supportive, encouraging arms around teenagers. And then I noticed a young lady just a row or two in front of me who had no adult with her yet. I walked up behind, slipped my arm around her shoulders, and began to quietly pray, trusting God for the translation. A few minutes later, the service was over. As the lights came up, the tall young lady turned toward me with what I can only describe as the light of Christ shining in her eyes. Graziella.

Transformed because Adriana, Derli, and a few followers practice the reality of dirty faith.

Tertiary Lives

We were in Chicago's O'Hare Airport. Susan looked over at me and saw the tears streaming down my face. Notebook in my lap, I was reading emails. "What's wrong?" she asked, real concern in her eyes. I stared blankly at the screen and then handed it to her.

An email from Philip, discussing some mostly mundane matters. Then, at the end, a devastating sentence: "When I got back, I found that Lucia was being prostituted."

Nooooo.

We had gotten to know then nine-year-old Lucia two years earlier. She lived with her mentally ill mother, two younger sisters, and a younger brother in abject poverty. When the torrential rains set in, sewage-filled water rushed down a steep hill and flowed eight inches deep through their scrap-wood shack. Bare wires with pirated electricity powered a pair of light bulbs and a small worn-out refrigerator. Twice we brought workers and propped up the walls that leaned almost a foot out of plumb. It was a frightening existence. But Lucia seemed above it all. Beautiful, spirited, sassy, with a quick laugh, usually giving orders. This one would make it; she would break the cycle.

"When I got back, I found that Lucia was being · prostituted."

No. Please, God, no.

I refused to believe it. Surely her mother, mentally ill and impoverished as she was, would not force Lucia into this. Could her mother's occasional boyfriend be responsible? Had one of the brothel owners in the slum kidnapped her?

It was true, but for none of those reasons. What happened to Lucia is deplorably common. She is desperately poor. Like any little girl, she wants better things in life: nicer clothes, better food, perhaps some special attention, and to be told she is pretty. Because Lucia is growing up in a cultural context that places no stigma on prostitution, she chose to barter the only thing she has: herself. In exchange for a new blouse or a good meal, she entered a lifestyle that will be ultimately and devastatingly destructive.

In her new independence, Lucia will find pain. She has committed an act of self-betrayal. She will discover that the readily available drugs of the slum assuage the pain, and soon she'll sink deeper into a cycle of despair. Without intervention, we know this will happen because we've seen it happen too many times.

A few months later, Philip and I sat on the scavenged furniture in Lucia's mother's shack. We had brought food for the family and a few surprises for Lucia, her two sisters, and her brother. Lucia's eyes were hollow, drawn. She shook her head at our offerings. "I don't play with toys anymore."

Loss of innocence in an eleven-year-old.
Millions of little girls begin a lifestyle of prostitution
without even knowing what they are doing. How do you
stop a child from prostituting herself when her community
tells her this is a perfectly acceptable means of providing
for herself and her family? When she enjoys more approval
and appreciation from her abusers than she has ever received at home? When selling herself is just a part of growing up?
This is difficult, very difficult. We can do something for
Lucia, and we have, and will continue to do so for her and
her siblings—but what do we do about the hundreds of
thousands, millions of girls like her around our world?

We have all seen the headlines and heard the stories.
Trafficking—understood as the taking of young children, usually girls but sometimes boys, from their homes
and exploiting them as prostitutes—is an affront to everything
decent, an assault on what almost all of us see as civilized, a
remnant from a time when human life was cheap and women
and children were chattel. We know it is dehumanizing, brazen
in its abject immorality, and evil almost beyond comprehension.
Getting worked up about this kind of trafficking comes easily,
and rightly so. We should be outraged, and often are, at the men
and women who destroy children's lives for their own gain and
at the depravity that makes it profitable.

But, if we really look at it, trafficking defined this way is
just the tip of the iceberg and a symptom of a much greater
problem. Ultimately, the problem is much more difficult to address—and challenges us at the very core of what it means to
be a follower of Christ.

This is *the* great evil of our generation, yet our response to
it has been muted.

Let's start by understanding what trafficking really is. Trafficking is not just what we hear in the heart-wrenching and emotionally coercive stories of kids who have been kidnapped from their homes, sold to traffickers by their parents, or lured away by the promise of a better life. Take a look at the United States' Victims of Trafficking and Violence Protection Act of 2000: Sex trafficking occurs any time "a commercial sex act is induced by force, fraud or coercion, or in which the person induced to perform such an act has not attained eighteen years of age."[1] Remember Ileana, whose story started this book? She was sold in the backyard by her mother. By definition, that is sex trafficking. Lucia? No one pushed her to make the choice she made, but, because the men of the *favela* paid her for sex and she is under eighteen, it's trafficking.

And this kind of sexual exploitation of children is far more pervasive, far more pernicious, and, tragically, far more difficult to address than the blatant stealing and selling of children for sex. It is evil in its stealth. Addressing it takes thoughtful life- and culture-changing Christian compassion. It truly takes dirty faith.

It is hard to overstate the depth and prevalence of the problem. In Cambodia, it is estimated that about one-third of all prostitutes are under eighteen.[2] In India, the federal police say around 1.2 million children are believed to be involved in prostitution.[3] Brazil is considered to have the worst child sex trafficking record after Thailand. Various international sources agree that from 250,000 to 500,000 children live as child prostitutes,[4] but other sources in Brazil put the number at up to two million children.

When a twelve-year-old girl comes to us at Hope, we start with the assumption that she has been sexually exploited. And that exploitation leaves its mark. We have many girls in our care who simply do not know how to relate to a man other than in a sexual manner. They have been taught since early,

early childhood that their only value is as sexual objects. They do not know how to hug a man without it being sexual. Every conversation begins with eyes cut to the side and what is thought to be a seductive smile.

A few years back I was in the *Moscou favela* with a film crew. The slum borders the federal prison in Campinas; most of the residents are the wives and children of the prisoners. There are very few men in the community, and everyone is desperately poor. We showed up with a small truckload of donated food and passed full boxes to the families while talking to them about their lives. As Jeremy, one of our videographers, and I walked through the *favela*, a group of young girls began mugging for the camera. Two of them were five or six years old, one maybe seven, the oldest probably eight or nine. Laughter, fast chatter, the general silliness endemic to children everywhere. After a few minutes, the younger girls wandered off, and there was an immediate change in the oldest girl. She slipped the strap of her dress off her shoulder, cut her eyes, and struck a nine-year-old's version of a seductive pose. A nine-year-old, modeling what she understood it means to be a woman. Jeremy immediately switched off the camera and turned away. If she was not already selling herself, she almost certainly is now.

The story is repeated over and over and over, throughout the world, in all types of cultures.

The vast majority of these kids will never make the headlines. They were not kidnapped. They were not shipped across international borders. They have not become the property of some trafficker. They are kids, just kids, surviving the only way they have available to them. No one tells them this is wrong. No one tells them their actions are destructive or warns them what the end will be. No ones cries for them. And yet this type of sexual trafficking is exactly what establishes the milieu that *does* give rise to the headline-grabbing stories of kidnapping, sex tourism, and sexual slavery. Were it not for acceptance of childhood prostitution as a way of life, we would never see the more blatant forms.

This is not okay just because there is no contextual condemnation of it. This is not okay because these children are less cherished, because they are not as clean and well-fed as the kid down the street—or the child in your home. This is not okay because innocence and purity aren't as valued in their community as in your church. This is wrong; it is evil at its core. It is not okay simply because that's just the way it is.

These are children, absolutely no different from your children or my children, or your brothers and sisters, and they are selling their bodies—or having their bodies stolen—every day, every night.

Ten million children worldwide.

We can't let the number overwhelm us. We can't let our eyes glaze over here. These are not nameless children who deserve no better. These are children created in the image of our Father, who loves them as much as he loves me or you or our children. And his heart is broken for every one of them.

Just as ours should be.

And if we take Scripture seriously, there's some accountability here. These are my brothers and sisters. If all that these kids rate is our shrug of indifference, those "depart from me" words come into play.

So What Do We Do About It?

How about we start to take it seriously? Do a web search for "anti-sex traffic organizations" and you will end up with nearly twenty million hits. Obviously, these do not represent distinct organizations, but there are a lot of people out there for whom stopping the sexual exploitation of children is really important.

But skim down the page. Are you struck, as I am, by how few Christian organizations are taking on this issue?

Look at a college campus, for example. Sex trafficking is a problem that concerns a lot of young adults. They care deeply about it. It strikes a chord to which they feel they must respond. But I want to be really clear about something here. We—the Church, not the college communities, not the world at large, not some pro-children organization—*we* have the answer for these kids, because we understand that the healing they desperately need involves more than a change in context or the promise of a job. Their hearts must be made whole.

I sat in the office of a missions pastor of a large church in the southern United States. We were talking about the church's interaction with a sizable children's residential shelter in Honduras. Many of the kids came from the world of sex trades. He talked about what a great place the shelter was, how the kids loved it there, how their smiles could change a life, but he was concerned by the metrics for the kids once they graduated. "It seems like every one of these kids goes right back to the way of life they had before they came to the home. If they came off the streets, they went right back to the streets. If a girl was a prostitute, she was selling herself six months after graduating. The home is simply not changing the outcomes for these kids. They are kept safe and happy for a few years, but then they go right back to where they came from."

We spent a few minutes talking about the campus, their vocational and academic programs, and how strong this aspect was. And then I asked the important question: What about the spiritual aspect of the program? "That has become a real problem for our church," the pastor truthfully responded. "We have some leadership that questions whether or not we should be supporting the shelter because it refuses to bring an evangelical component into the program."

Cause and effect, perhaps?

Transformation is what the Church brings to the table. A few years ago, NBC sent a film crew to Brazil to briefly tell Hope's story as part of their "Making a Difference" news feature. They talked about the life of street kids, told a bit of our history, looked at our academic and vocational programs. Then near the end of the segment, Bob Faw narrates, "It is a real mixture here, job skills and education and tough love. But what Hope Unlimited has learned is that that combination only goes so far." Then a cut to kids in a worship service. "Kids here also learn that the spiritual is foremost." Philip onscreen concludes, "The parenting stuff goes a long way with some of them, but in some cases, without God, they are just not going to change."[5]

That's it. That is the difference—the specific component we as the Church can offer that no one else brings to the table. Children with such pasts need alternatives to their only way of making a living; they need safety, family. But more than anything else, they need the healing that only comes from the Father of love.

This is a special kind of redemption, taking those who often see themselves as unsalvageable and helping them reclaim their lives. Taking those whom the world has proclaimed to be objects for others' gratification and helping them see themselves as created in the image of the living God and worthy of *his* love.

In the midst of introducing these kids to the first father they have ever known to love them and want the best for them, we can also help them reclaim their childhood, their innocence.

A story: Around Valentine's Day every year, churches, individuals, families, and elementary school classes include Hope Unlimited in their celebrations. We receive hundreds and hundreds of Valentine cards addressed to our girls in Brazil. Philip and I show up on campus with duffel bags stuffed with every shape and form of card imaginable. Then we turn the tables on

Brazil's Day of Love, a very secular, very carnal celebration of love held on June 12. Our staff, and perhaps a visiting friend or two, gather the girls, pass out the cards, and start a conversation about what love really is, what it means to be chaste and pure, and how God can heal a heart shattered by years of betrayal and abuse.

As I heard one of our girls pray, "Father, I thank you that you have made me pure again."

We. *We* have the answer.

So back to the question: Why isn't taking care of these kids, transforming their lives, and recapturing their innocence a burning, consuming drive of the Church? These kids are the definition of the least of these. So why do we take a backseat to the rest of the world when it comes to advocacy for sexually exploited kids?

That's a difficult question, and the answer has a lot of layers to it. One piece of the puzzle lies in the fact that this is hard work, with no guarantees of success. It is one thing to provide the food for an impoverished family, or to teach kids a craft that will enable them to change their lives, or even to adopt an infant who will become a part of your family. It is a completely different order of difficulty to transform the life of a fourteen-year-old girl who has been selling her body for five years. The "product" is not as appealing, there's a lot more baggage, and truth be known, we don't feel like we are dealing with an innocent child. So we bypass these kids.

Given the right circumstances, would you adopt a baby? Probably so. Your investment over sixteen years? Around $250,000. But would you be willing to exert the same amount of effort and money to change the life of a teenage prostitute?

Please do not misunderstand me here. Every one of those easy fixes is something we ought to be doing, but remember in chapter 2 when we talked about why we do what we do? That plays out here, on both the corporate and individual levels. If we are being obedient to God for the sake of obedience, then the natural inclination is going to be for us to act out that obedience in the easiest way possible. Even if there is enough commitment and conviction that we engage the least of these, we want to write the check, send the mission team, or adopt the program that most immediately and easily assuages our conscience. But there is a difference here between obedience for obedience's sake and the passion for these kids that is an outgrowth of the love God places in our hearts.

So play it a different way. What if our motivation is not to rack up successful transformations or to chart the quickest route to obedience, or even just to do something that makes us feel good—what if our motivation comes from a wellspring of God-birthed love? What if we are genuinely viewing all these kids as God does, seeing in every one of them the image of our Creator? What if overflowing love shapes everything we do?

We'll practice dirty faith. And we will practice it for the victims of sexual exploitation. This chapter is not about being able to tell the most compelling story of a sex-trafficked child, although many of their stories will absolutely grab you. The capture of your heart for this issue should take place on a much higher plane. This is between you and God. And from where I sit, it is a marker of faith and grace. *My cup overflows and splashes grace on everyone around me.*

Again, What Do We Do About It?

So, what now? The beginning point is that we get our own house in order. This is a spiritual battle, and it is fought at the very highest level. Why don't we get this as Christians? Far too often, we want to fight the symptom rather than deal with root causes. Where do we find the moral and spiritual authority to challenge the world about its notion of accepted sexual mores and the sexual objectification of children? Please understand, the world at large really does not have a problem with sexualized children.

A few years ago, a hotel in which I was staying in Brazil was hosting "The Search for the Next Giselle." The hotel lobby had a thirty-foot-high banner of the Brazilian supermodel, dress cut to midriff, skirt blown up to thighs, advertising the upcoming event. Soon the hotel lobby would be filled with beautiful Brazilian models, right?

Not what happened. When the day of interviews arrived, I was shocked to see not seventeen- or twenty-year-olds, but mothers bringing their eight- or ten-year-old daughters, overly made-up and underdressed. I wanted to grab them and point to the posters and say, "Is this what you want for your daughter? You want to sell your ten-year-old as a sex object?" But I didn't because I realized that was exactly what they wanted.

And how different are we? More and more, we Christians have become ambivalent to matters of sexual morality. We give a passing nod to biblical teaching about purity, but is it a priority? The secular perspective is so pervasive that it no longer even draws a response from us. From all appearances, this is a battle where we have surrendered, and we are paying the price for it in our communities, churches, and homes.

Let's look at the context here. In a world of moral relativism, in a world where prostitution is a "victimless crime," in a world where any statement about biblical morality is a rearguard action, the exploitation of children is inevitable. If there are no right and wrong answers, we cannot make the case to protect the most vulnerable. And the whole question of context starts in our own hearts; the battle is enjoined in obedience. Then— *then*—we have the spiritual platform to challenge the world.

To change the world, we must change our hearts.

This is the point at which we need to be the Church. One voice, consistently and constantly speaking truth to the evil that is the sexual exploitation of children. *We have to talk about this.* It is not a comfortable Sunday morning conversation. It is offensive, not polite. But perhaps, just perhaps, one Sunday we could sit in the pews and reflect on what happened to millions of little girls, little boys, and teenagers around the world the night before. Look around your church. What if the kids you see were the ones fighting to survive the abuse? Would we make time to talk about them?

The great challenge here is that we have to change a cultural context. Saving the kids already trapped in the business is critically important, but ending the practice is the ultimate agenda. And that means changing the way a community—a world—looks at children.

Remember when we talked in chapter 3 about spiritual authority? This is where that abstract conversation meets the concrete reality of the world. When we truly are the Church, we have a platform from which to name evil what it is. And the power to transform the context for these kids is explicitly the same power that Jesus, Peter, and James called on. Spiritual authority always trumps the material. "You, dear children, are from God and have overcome them, because the one who is in you is greater than the one who is in the world" (1 John 4:4). I want you to really get this: We cannot change a world that turns a blind eye to—or worse yet, actively participates in—the prostitution of children. But God can.

Mas Deus.

But words must beget activity, and this is not the sort of easy thing an individual church can fix. That's not a blanket statement. Some churches, in some settings, have extraordinary ministries rescuing kids who are living the nightmare of child prostitution. But most children trapped in the world of trafficking are beyond the reach of a local church; the local church rarely has the expertise or ability to address this problem. What we can do is empower the followers who are actively engaged in fighting this battle. And there are some serious followers out there who are standing on the front lines, not just calling evil for what it is, but taking children by the hand and leading them out of prostitution and into safe, pure, productive, and fulfilling lives. Followers like Adriana, the social worker in Campinas. Like Ralph Borde and the group he founded, As Our Own, rescuing girls in the brothels of New Delhi. Redeemed lives. Transformed lives.

Does your church budget specifically provide funding for an organization rescuing children from the sex trades? Does your family budget? The work many followers of Christ do with these children is the essence of dirty faith. It is difficult, very difficult. It is expensive. Buying a daily cup of rice and beans for a little girl who is supporting herself and her siblings by selling her body in a local bar does not cut it. It takes serious investment in her life—the same kind of commitment and investment it would take to bring a child into your home. And we need to be standing shoulder-to-shoulder with the people who are meeting this challenge head-on.

Be outraged. Now.

Do something. Now. Invest in the followers who are making a difference in the lives of these children.

Because transformation can happen.

A story: I met nineteen-year-old Tatiani at the same time I met Janai, her eight-year-old daughter. That's not a misprint: nineteen-year-old mom, eight-year-old daughter. When Tatiani was nine, her mother, a prostitute, began selling her. Just after she turned eleven, Tatiani became pregnant. When the baby was born, her mother instructed Tatiani to get rid of the child because she was bad for business. Tatiani, unwilling to abandon her baby, found an older woman in the *favela* who was willing to raise the child. Not long afterward, Tatiani was taken into custody and brought to the City of Youth. The twelve-year-old insisted to the social workers that she had a baby named Janai, who was living in the slum. Disbelieving at first, our staff investigated, found the older woman, and found Janai. It was determined that the best place for the baby was to stay where she was, but our social workers would provide support, and Tatiani would have the chance for supervised weekend visits with her daughter. They could not let her make the visit alone, because she herself was still in danger from her mother and the others in the slum who had trafficked her. But she had the chance to bond and be part of the little girl's life.

Fast forward a few years. Tatiani graduated from Hope, got a good job, and established her own home. The woman in the slum was aging quickly, her health was failing, and taking care of a little girl was becoming more than she could handle. So Janai came to live with her mother—her birth mother. And now there is a dad on the scene and a little brother. And this is a godly young family. The prospects for her children are so different from what they were a decade ago for Tatiani because someone made a place for a twelve-year-old prostitute to have her life transformed.

In Prison,
and You Visited Me

I had been warned that going into the children's prison at
Cariacica would be difficult. We visited at night. I tried
to prepare myself for the sights, smells, and sounds of the
place, but I was still shocked. The physical and spiritual
darkness was oppressive. A barren, crumbling cement
building housed the children in windowless cells with no
running water, bathing facilities, heat, or fresh air. Toilets
were holes in the cement floor. Some cells held up to five
kids behind heavy steel doors. No medical or dental care
was provided. The darkness was punctuated by a single,
naked light bulb hanging in about half of the cells—the
only light we saw.

In this gloom, it was hard to believe that the dark forms
that approached the steel bars were human. Yet as we
talked and prayed with the kids, most seemed desperate to
begin a new life, to be given another chance. They were

longing for a touch, a handshake, or any encouragement. Yet they were utterly hopeless that their lives could ever change. As hard as going in was, walking out, leaving them in darkness, was even harder. I did not sleep well that night, haunted by the images of caged children.

—Dr. Burt McDowell

"When did we see you hungry and feed you, or thirsty and give you something to drink? When did we see you a stranger and invite you in, or needing clothes and clothe you? When did we see you sick or in prison and go to visit you?" The King will reply, "Truly I tell you, whatever you did for one of the least of these brothers and sisters of mine, you did for me."

Matthew 25:37–40

In Brazil, an estimated fourteen thousand children are incarcerated in unspeakably subhuman conditions. In the Congo, three thousand children live behind bars, food supplies are sporadically provided by family from the outside—otherwise the kids just go hungry.[1] In Yemen, a U.N. report found that even when children held in Sana'a Central Prison finish their sentences, they remain in prison due to their inability to pay court-imposed fines.[2] In Russia's sixty-plus children's prison camps, an estimated fourteen thousand kids live under inhumane conditions behind concrete walls and barbed wire.[3] Often, they do not have proper shoes or clothes to endure the harsh Russian winters.

Worldwide, UNICEF tags the number at 1.1 million children behind bars.[4]

Are these bad kids? Yep. Murderers? Yes. Rapists, drug dealers, kidnappers? Without question.

And we are called to be the hands of the Christ who loves them.

A Bit of Theological Digression Here . . .

To begin, a question for you: What was the last interaction Jesus had with a person before his death? *Truly I tell you, today you will be with me in paradise.* The thief being crucified beside him. His words were not a panacea handed to a lost cause. This was acceptance, forgiveness, redemption. No accident here.

You will hear a lot about forgiveness in these pages—because eyes open at the heart level.

This is a tough one. If we are to be completely honest, I think most of us will admit to having a problem with the above Scripture. Not the stranger or sick part, and certainly not the hungry and thirsty part. Perhaps not even the naked part. We get those. It is absolutely intrinsic to who we are as followers of Christ to take care of those who have been given a raw deal by life. But there is one more condition on the checklist in this passage that makes most of us pretty uncomfortable.

I was in prison and you visited me.

Orphans? Of course. Hungry children? Absolutely. Kids who have been trafficked? Certainly.

Prisoners?

These kids are not the warm, soft-focus pictures of the children God called us to serve.

Look at the others—the non-prisoners—whom Jesus called "the least of these"; you can understand and sympathize with their plights. If someone is hungry or thirsty, or if they are in need of clothes, or if they are sick or strangers, we should act in Christian charity (1 Corinthians 13 again!) toward them. Bottom line, most of these people are in circumstances imposed by someone else, not something necessarily caused by their own choices. At the very least, they are victims, perhaps of their own bad choices, but they certainly are not showing malicious intent toward others.

Prisoners are a different matter. As a friend said to me recently, "My perspective is, if they are in prison, they probably belong there." And he is right. Society, if it wants to survive, cannot give a free pass to those who choose to violate its standards of behavior, and so we start with the shared affirmation that when laws are broken, penalty is necessary, and certain crimes are so egregious that penal confinement is requisite. We all understand this.

There is no evidence that Jesus ever questioned the need for jails or prisons, but he nonetheless included the prisoner in his recital of those for whom we are to care. How can we understand this directive? After all, he seems pretty serious about it; the rejoinder in Matthew 25:41–43 (RSV)—"Depart from me, you cursed, into the eternal fire prepared for the devil and his angels; for I was hungry and you gave me no food, I was thirsty and you gave me no drink, I was a stranger and you did not welcome me, naked and you did not clothe me, sick and in prison and you did not visit me"—does not carve out an exception for those behinds bars.

We have a few choices in how to approach this. Perhaps Jesus was speaking in some kind of holy hyperbole, naming every type of person who came to mind with a bit of righteous exaggerating just to get our attention. Or perhaps, given the political context of the day, he was slipping in a seditious shot at the Roman overlords; maybe the prisoners to whom he referred were unjustly jailed for their political views.

Probably not. There is nothing in the text to support either of those approaches. I think Jesus meant exactly what he said. Funny how he did that so often. *I was sick and in prison and you visited me.* So how do we get our arms around this one? Why add criminals to the mix?

I think the key begins here: *There is no gradation of sin.* "While we were still sinners, Christ died for us" (Romans 5:8). Jesus never looked at the prisoner and said, "You know, there is a qualitative difference between a prisoner's sin and the sin of my followers." We are all alienated from God because of sin in our lives, and before experiencing the saving grace of Jesus, I was as much a stranger to God as a death row inmate.

You were as much a stranger to God as the rapist, murderer, thief, and drug dealer. We are *all* prisoners—some of our own devices, shackled by sin, some of the state.

But Christ loves us anyway.

The qualitative difference is not between us and the child behind bars. It is between us and God. But that span does not stop the engulfing love of God. Paul said, "Neither height nor depth, nor anything else in all creation, will be able to separate us from the love of God that is in Christ Jesus our Lord" (Romans 8:39).

Jesus never loves just the lovable. His love is not conditioned by the status of its object. When Jesus sees someone hurting, even if the pain is self-inflicted, his reaction is to extend grace.

He demands his followers do the same.

Over the past few years, I have spent significant time thinking about what it means to be a follower of Christ rather than just a really good person—besides the very obvious saved-by-grace, of course. I mean, how do I act differently, specifically, because I am a follower of Jesus of Nazareth? This may be one of those points of divergence when it comes to prisoners—even child prisoners.

You do not like these kids just because you have a good heart. There is nothing here that calls to us in the same way as the hungry little boy or the trafficked girl. Kids in prison are rarely pretty, or even pitiful. They are usually street-hardened thugs, anger dominant in their eyes. They've done bad things, perhaps really bad things. The bars are only one of the obstacles separating them from us.

But Jesus loves them, and if—*if*—our lives have been transformed by his grace, we love them, too.

So I stand in the very clean, fully equipped auto body repair shop at our Hope Mountain campus. The students have on their spotless, pressed uniforms identifying them as trainees in the program. They are different from most of the kids who come from the neighborhood because they know they have prospects in life; there is a waiting list to hire our graduates for good-paying jobs.

I look about a half mile or so across a lush valley to the starkly whitewashed but deteriorating walls of the children's prison at Cariacica, the same place Dr. McDowell described at the beginning of this chapter. Four weeks earlier, the Organization of American States' Human Rights Court had issued a formal indictment against the nation of Brazil for conditions in its children's prisons. The report singled out one prison for the brutality of its conditions: Cariacica. Children killed inside the prison. At our doorstep. *I was sick and in prison and you visited me.*

Really dirty faith.

Children's Prisons?

Yes, prisons. We are not talking about juvenile detention centers where kids are sent when they are expelled from school (although being concerned about kids in those situations is not a bad idea, either). We are talking about prisons, places worse than anything adult offenders ever see in the United States or in the Eurozone.

Children's prisons. Oppressive places. How do kids even get there? Lots of ways. Many children are there for what human rights organizations call "crimes of status." Prostitution (legal for adults in many, if not most, developing countries), truancy, or even just being on the streets without a home can place children behind bars for "crimes" that are legally permissible for adults. Sometimes kids are essentially imprisoned simply because they are kids.

In other cases, children go to prison for crimes committed by adults. It works like this: In Brazil, for example, juveniles who commit even heinous crimes are released when they turn eighteen. So an adult gang member commits a crime, then goes to a fifteen-year-old with an ultimatum: "You take the fall, or we will kill your family." The teenager confesses, is sentenced, and then spends three years behind bars learning how to be a *real* criminal.

However, while it is possible a child is on the wrong side of a political battle or is imprisoned just to get them out of the way, oftentimes kids are behind bars because they have committed acts of violence. They have robbed, murdered, raped, and/or kidnapped. No soft-pedaling of their circumstances can change this fact.

By and large, these kids are criminals. *Seriously, Jesus?* Do we really want—or have—to get into that?

I was sick and in prison and you visited me. Sometimes, just sometimes, don't you wish Jesus could have been a little more generic in what he commands us to do? Perhaps *Love the Lord your God with all your heart, and be nice to people.* Or even if he had just not gone into detail—by both teaching and example—of how he expects us to love our neighbors.

But we are talking about children here. There is no way we as the Church can be sitting on the sidelines when children— *children*—live in these conditions. Our acceptance of their status absolutely makes a lie of our confession of the transforming grace brought to us in Jesus Christ. *Jesus changed me, but these kids are beyond his reach.*

One of the amazing things about the way God works is that he takes us where we are and works in our hearts and contexts to get us where we need to be. Over a decade ago, Hope Unlimited opened Hope Mountain, a residential program for street boys in Vitória. The campus is the one right across the valley from the children's prison at Cariacica. It is an absolutely beautiful facility with an extraordinary backdrop of the eponymous rain-forest-covered mountain, a soccer field, a swimming pool, and state-of-the-art vocational facilities. It is truly a world-class children's shelter serving a population in desperate need.

We were completely convinced God had placed us there, and we opened with good funding from the U.S. and strong backing from the local juvenile authorities. Some of our older kids from Campinas even made the move up to the new campus to help us establish the positive culture we had learned was critical to the transformation of young lives.

Then we floundered for an entire decade. As costs skyrocketed in Brazil, the exchange rate plummeted. Silicon Valley, the source of much of our U.S. support, dried up financially with the dot-com crash. Our ministry model calls for developing indigenous support for all of our programming, but, even as they sang our praises for work with their street kids, local officials made no funding available to us. After ten years, Hope Mountain was on the verge of collapse. We were pouring money into a deteriorating program to such an extent that it was threatening the survival of the entire organization.

The same day that the Organization of American States' Human Rights Court issued the judgment against the children's prisons in Brazil, we announced we would be closing Hope Mountain. It was not a decision that came easily, and it was one that made us really question our understanding of God's leadership. Our board chair said to me, "I do not understand this; it was so clear to us that God wanted us here, but it has been one trial after another. And now this."

Then God stepped in. We were summoned to a meeting with the vice-governor of the state—on the day we were scheduled to close. Ten minutes after the official closing time, the vice-governor made an extraordinary offer: The state would provide full funding to keep Hope Mountain open, if—and this is a really important *if*—we would agree to help them with the problems they were having in their children's prisons. Would we be willing to take some boys out of the prisons and give them a chance at Hope Mountain? And if we were able to continue operating Hope Mountain, would we develop a proposal to completely re-envision the state's juvenile detention program, to give the kids a chance to be transformed rather than condemned to a life of crime?

Of course we would.

A few months later, I posed a question to our board: If things at Hope Mountain had been running smoothly for a decade, if we had all the funding we needed, if local support covered any gaps, if the campus was full and thriving, would we have been at all open to starting a difficult work with children prisoners? Heads shook around the room, with a few quietly mouthing, "No." Maybe those years in the desert were just to get us to where God wants us to be.

And that is the wonderful thing about dirty faith. God does not just send us; he travels with us. *A cloud of smoke by day, a pillar of fire by night.* Or maybe, just maybe, simply a constant awareness of his presence as we move through the deserts of our lives.

Forgiveness

How even to tell this story, a story about how God puts our hearts right? It starts with an email to a dear friend of almost four decades, asking her permission to use a story that is intensely

personal. Her gracious—and astonishingly joyful—permission.
And then a follow-up email to her father, asking him not only
for permission, but also for him to recount his part of the story
in his words. This story:

Many years ago, when Michelle was in her early twenties, her
parents, returning home from a midweek Bible study at their
church, were jumped by four men and beaten senseless with
tire tools. Hearing her parents' screams, Michelle ran outside
their home and was abducted by the men in the family van.
As church members gathered with her parents at the hospital,
Michelle was brutally assaulted, and her kidnappers began to
talk in front of her of the best way to kill her. Intense prayer at
the hospital. Miraculously, the men decided to release her, hand
her the van keys, and walk away. Deliverance. Prayer answered.

But that is only the first chapter of the story. This family was
hurt badly, terribly. Physically, emotionally, spiritually wounded.
Visible wounds; much more profound wounds deep beneath
the surface. I'll let Michelle's dad pick up the story from there:

> After I knew our daughter was safe and I had some sem-
> blance of consciousness about me, I began the process of
> formulating a plan to extract revenge upon the perpetra-
> tors. I owned a construction company and was already
> aware of the necessity of having a plan to complete pro-
> jects. My next project was going to involve those four men
> who had exacted such misery and devastation upon my
> family. I felt very responsible for what happened. I was
> supposed to keep them safe, and I didn't keep the "weak-
> est" members safe from physical harm. I also "knew" that
> this nightmare was because of my sin and sinful thoughts,
> and I knew my daughter and wife had experienced pain.
> I really had not experienced any pain because the initial
> blow of the attack left me unconscious.

The only problem I had as I formulated my plan of revenge was the constant intervention of God upon my thinking. I was never completely able to dismiss God from my thoughts. As I made plans, he would intervene, and I knew that what I was even thinking about was wrong. I wanted it so bad that—as I was torn between what I wanted and what I knew God wanted—I had spells of crying. Our oldest son thought I had some sort of post-stress reaction to the attack. He had the hospital chaplain come and talk with me, but this didn't accomplish anything because I already knew what the problem was. I just didn't want to deal with it.

Never during this time did the Bible verse "'Vengeance is mine,' says the Lord" come to mind. Basically, just the thought of God himself not approving of what I was entertaining to do was the intervention that kept invading my plan. This would bring on a time of crying, and eventually his intervention became so strong that I knew I would have to give up my plan. Then, one day when I was still lying in the hospital, I had a dream that I had just crossed the Jordan River, and as I set foot on the bank, I thought about the ones who had harmed me; they were on the side I had just come from. As I was turning to go back to implement my plan of revenge, God spoke to me, telling me that if I went back, I would never return to where I was supposed to be. He said that I knew where I was supposed to be, and it wasn't on the other side of the river. I looked across the river and realized that "across the river" was not for me. I didn't want to be like Lot's wife, so I turned forward and looked at the ground before me, the Promised Land God had laid out.

The point here? When Jesus instructed us to care for the least of these, his concern was as much for us as it was for the orphan, the widow, the hungry, the prisoner. When we as individuals, or collectively as the Church, withhold the grace of forgiveness, when we claim the blood right, when we define or identify the transgressor by his transgressions, the damage is not just to their lives, it is also to our souls.

Does society have a right, an obligation, to punish criminals? Absolutely. But even as society acts to enforce its laws and hold accountable those who violate them, as followers of Christ, we must seek the redemption and transformation of the prisoner. And that redemption begins in forgiveness, because without forgiveness, there can be no relationship.

Dirty faith . . . and cleansing grace.

And You Visited Me

This is not about showing up on Saturday at the local jail and checking "visit" off our obedience list. In Scripture, visitation always carries the idea not only of presence but also of activity. For the arrogant, for the self-righteous, for the oppressor, presence brought judgment. Hosea 9:7 (KJV) says, "The days of visitation are come, the days of recompence are come." But for the oppressed, for the least of these, presence means deliverance: "Blessed be the Lord God of Israel; for he hath visited and redeemed his people" (Luke 1:68 KJV).

We are not to be people who just show up at an appointed family-and-friends time at the local jail. That's not dirty; that's easy. We are to be agents of transformation, difference-makers. Our visitation is to be a time of delivering grace, and in grace is embedded hope. Please get this: When Jesus said, "I was sick and in prison and you visited me," he was not handing us a pattern for good deeds. He was instructing us to be the vessels by which the sick and the prisoner experience his grace, and in that experience have the trajectory of their lives—their eternities—radically redirected.

Does God hold us accountable for our indifference here? Over one million children in prison, in unimaginably inhumane conditions, and it is not even a blip on the Church's radar? At your next Bible study group or Sunday school class, toss out that number and see if you get more than a shrug. We have enough beautiful, happy children who need homes; why bother with criminals?

Depart from me. . . . I was sick and in prison and you did not look after me.

This is a really tough one—one that challenges us at the very core of what it means to be a follower of Jesus. And embedded in the issue is a related question: How can the Church engage in really large-scale concerns? How do we, as churches and as individual believers, address the issues that seem beyond us, the questions too big for us to answer?

The first step is that we begin to think, act, and *obey* like the Church, rather than as unconnected, essentially isolated local communities of believers. Think back about five hundred years. The Church had abandoned both its moral and spiritual authority, essentially commercializing grace. One man, the German monk Martin Luther, challenged the Church to begin taking Scripture and grace seriously. But the Reformation happened, not just because one man had the courage to stand up to a religious plutocracy, but because his message found resonance with the hearts and minds of the people of the Church. Remember the parable of the sower? The good soil happened there. Luther's message of the primacy of Scripture and the sufficiency of grace spread like wildfire through Europe because the hearts of God's people were ready to receive it.

Five hundred years later, we need a new Reformation, one that calls us to remember and to understand that God's grace is not the province of a privileged few. It is the vessel of transformation for a desperate world, and it calls us as the Church to get really animated about what this grace can do for those imprisoned by sin or the laws of their land. We become the instruments of Isaiah 61:1: "The Spirit of the Sovereign Lord is on me, because the Lord has anointed me to proclaim good news to the poor. He has sent me to bind up the brokenhearted, to proclaim freedom for the captives and release from darkness for the prisoners."

Leaking grace? We need to do that right here, at this very spot. If God's grace has truly captured us, the call to set prisoners free will resonate in our hearts. Not every follower of Christ will walk into a children's prison; not all of us will run programs to give juvenile offenders a chance at life; most will not challenge the systems that lock children up in dehumanizing conditions. But it will be on each of our hearts, our minds, and our tongues. We will care about this, and every one of us will support those who are on the front lines fighting the spiritual battles in this realm of darkness.

And then we will trust God for the outcomes. In every generation, whenever the people of God have collectively gotten serious about faithfulness to his call, he has moved individuals to become the hands of his ministry. When our hearts are in the right place, he will provide a Luther, a Zwingli, a Knox, a Tyndale. Of this I am certain: God loves those in prison as deeply as he loves you or me. The issue for us is whether our experience of his love is deep enough that such love can flow through us to them—replicating the love of Christ to those the world has condemned.

Dirty faith, defined.

PART THREE

COMMUNITY

The Echo of God's Love

I do not like this chapter. Not at all.

But it is necessary. You see, as believers, we are not just called to be compassionate, we are also called to have wisdom. Wisdom doesn't come easily, and it is often accompanied by pain, by discomfort. But in it there may also be a new level of faith and a different kind of obedience— obedience in a place where we learn the difference between activities that make us feel good and activities that actually do good.

Let me give you an example. Thailand has a horrific market in child slavery. Kids are bought and sold, usually as a part of the sex trade. You come up with a really great idea to save some of these kids: Purchase them before the sex traffickers do, then put them in foster care or place them for adoption.

Great idea; saves kids from a horrible future, right? God's work here.

Maybe not. What if your good intentions create a new market for children, give the sex traffickers a new cover, and create a rationale for families with no resources or ways to care for their own kids to give children up to the marketers? And for every child you save, you push two or maybe three into the market? It happens.

Or, an example that's closer to home. Your church wants to take a first dip in this taking-care-of-the-least-of-these pool. You set up a program where low-income families can come to the church office and get some help with their electric bills, or perhaps a voucher for groceries. You extend the grace of Jesus toward them.

Or do you? Perhaps what you actually do is ingrain bad spending habits. Or worse, perhaps you deepen the gulf of status between the provider and the recipient of the gift, and you perpetuate a cycle of poverty. It happens, too.

Really good intentions. Really, really bad outcomes.

We have to think about these things, talk about them. I have a real concern that we as followers are too often looking for an easy out, a way of passing off responsibility—and this concern about impacts is a tailor-made excuse for inaction. Acknowledging this problem takes a really mature faith, one that can truly "correctly handle the word of truth." Bottom line here: This is not a prescription for inaction. It is a demand for even more diligent, more difficult activity.

I hope you are hurting by the time you get to this chapter, that your encounter with the least of these over the previous chapters has absolutely boiled your heart to make things different—transformative—for them. I hope you read the words here looking for a way that truly seeks to re-create the transforming ministry of Christ.

To begin our search for that way, let's phrase the question differently: When is doing good actually harmful, and how do we as followers of Christ act in a manner that truly improves the lot of the least of these?

The answer is not immediately an easy one. It is an answer that sometimes leads us away from our best instincts and requires our heads to temper our hearts. But, please hear this: Concern for outcomes is never an excuse for inactivity. In fact, it is just the opposite. It is a call to action, an action driven not only by a caring heart but also godly wisdom.

When you look at the stories of the Gospels, the ministry of Jesus was intentionally focused on transformation. Did he "fix" the physical, the material? Absolutely, but he did so consistently within the context of changing a life. We can find the occasional occurrence where Jesus met a short-term need—feeding the five thousand comes to mind—but in the large majority of cases, he was altering the context of a person's existence; the blind saw, the paralytic walked, and, most important, those with soul sickness encountered the transforming love of the Savior.

Here is an extended project for you. Read through one of the Gospels, looking in particular at Jesus' interaction with people in need. See if you can find a case where he heals or forgives but you worry that he might really be perpetuating the problem. I can't find one. His interaction was always focused beyond the moment of encounter, always seeking to transform a life.

In the same way, we absolutely must engage in caring for the hurting of the world. The need for social justice is unimaginably huge. We have run through the numbers already; our world is full of hungry, exploited, abused, and abandoned children. In response, our encounter with the living Savior and his grace compels us to be engaged in their lives.

But we have to do it the right way. We must make the choices that make a difference. We cannot throw money at a problem, feel good about it, and then walk away—responsibility resolved, guilt absolved. That is not Christian charity. Our love and activity for those in need must always take place within the context of our relationship with Jesus Christ. First Corinthians 13:13 (KJV): "Now abideth faith, hope, charity." The three are not unrelated but are the composite of who he is and who we are to be. Faith is the conviction not of God's existence, but of his benevolent activity in our lives. Hope is the belief, based on the evidence of that faith, that he will continue to act *for* us. Charity—love—is our activity based on faith and hope; it is the echo of God's love in our own lives. The subsequent always flows out of its antecedent.

So when we get busy with the activity of grace in the world, the focus is always beyond us, always on bringing others to the point of experiencing God in the same way we do. Dirty faith echoes.

Here is a good operational question whenever we want to act in love toward others: *Will doing this allow them to become vessels of grace toward others as I am a vessel of grace toward them?*

Act

I am going to keep repeating this one because we must get it right: Don't sit on the sidelines. Act.

We can proof-text just about any position we want out of Scripture, and that is especially true when it comes to taking a pass on caring for the poor or homeless. "The one who is unwilling to work shall not eat" (2 Thessalonians 3:10). "The poor you will always have with you" (Matthew 26:11). We even canonize Ben Franklin: "God helps those who help themselves."

Concern that we are going to make a problem worse is never an excuse for inactivity. If, in fact, our hearts are in the right

116

place, if we are acting not out of some obligatory obedience/ responsibility complex, if we truly are overflowing vessels of grace, the challenge, nuance, or subtlety of a right answer will never be a deterrent to doing *something*. Inactivity because of concern over impacts says a lot more about our hearts than it does our minds.

So act.

Approaching this issue with both the mind and heart of God requires really pure motives. When we step back from doing good and think deeply, discerningly, *wisely* about what we are doing, it must never be because we are looking to pawn off our involvement, but rather because we are always in search of more meaningful and deeper engagement.

Where Is the Focus?

One problem we see far too often is that Christian good works are much more about the worker than the receiver. Remember the remark a couple of chapters back about how much need there is in Orlando? *Really?* It seems we want to communicate to our youth that central to the idea of extending God's grace to those in need is that we have a very good time while doing it. True service becomes an afterthought, and true servanthood rarely enters the equation.

In the same way, virtually every mission trip—if it is a "one and done" situation, if there are no long-term relationships developed, if there is not at least some degree of reciprocity— amounts to little more than social tourism and has virtually nothing to do with the good news of transformation that Jesus brought to every encounter. It is let-me-feel-good-about-myself charity. As Paul said, "So I find this law at work: Although I want to do good, evil is right there with me" (Romans 7:21). But the prophet Isaiah points us in a different direction: "If you spend yourselves in behalf of the hungry and satisfy the needs of the oppressed, then your light will rise in the darkness, and your night will become like the noonday" (Isaiah 58:10). *Spend yourselves.* I like that.

Wrong motives and poorly conceived charity damages both the giver and the recipient of the gift. The bottom line is that the heartfelt, emotional basis of our good intentions can mislead us about what is truly helpful for others. We have to be very careful here. We like our privilege and position. We embrace the image of who we are when we give, when we truly are the *noblesse.* And if we are not careful, generosity can reinforce our very worst instincts (not to mention the bad effects it can have on the objects of our largesse). In doing good, we end up doing wrong. Paul had a take on it this way: "If I give all I possess to the poor and give over my body to hardship that I may boast, but do not have love, I gain nothing." Then he described the foundation for doing good: "Love is patient, love is kind. It does not envy, it does not boast, it is not proud. It does not dishonor others, it is not self-seeking . . ." (1 Corinthians 13:3–5). He was on to something there.

For the wealthy—and that's all of us—serving others can reinforce our intuition that we are where we are because we deserve to be here. *Giving forgives any debt of grace we have incurred.* The "feel good" aspect of Christian charity work can be intoxicating, and it plays to all our base instincts.

This is the way Satan works: The greatest temptations are always perversions—sometimes very slight perversions—of God's best for us. Look at the list: sexual impurity, born in the great gift of sexual intimacy that God provides for husband and wife; greed, a twisting of the sense of material blessing when God provides bountifully for us; spiritual pride, a turning of the humility that comes of being chosen by God to receive his gift of grace. And spiritual temptation can really play out in generosity. Giving to others can be spiritual poison.

I find it telling how quickly Jesus gets to this. In Matthew's account of the life of Jesus, Jesus takes a significant part of his first major sermon to say: "Take heed that you do not do your charitable deeds before men, to be seen by them. Otherwise you have no reward from your Father in heaven" (Matthew 6:1 NKJV). Then he goes a step further: "But when you do a charitable deed, do not let your left hand know what your right hand is doing" (Matthew 6:3 NKJV). Perhaps a little metaphoric hyperbole there, but he is really driving home the point that we better make sure our motives are right even when we are serving others. More on this in a minute or two.

But first, the flip side of the coin: For the poor, for the person receiving the gift, our good works can reinforce inferiority and bring increased dependence. In many cases, the impoverished, the disenfranchised, those living on the fringes of society carry deep, very negative images of themselves. Their self-perceived inferiority often paralyzes them into patterns of living that make it impossible for them to break the cycles of poverty and dependence. If we are not careful, a good Christian handout, instead of being a hand up, becomes a hand of oppression, reinforcing the chains of self-image.

So how do we make this work? How do we make the echo of God's love in our lives transformative for others?

The answer starts with our focus. What are we trying to do, and why are we trying to do it? Here's the secret: It's not about us. *But when you do a charitable deed, do not let your left hand know what your right hand is doing.* Our focus, from square one, is to love others in a way that brings transformation into *their* lives. We act intentionally, in channels that are not always the easiest to navigate, in order to see outcomes of truly changed lives.

There is a very basic difference in the way we usually do missions and the way God engages us through grace: *God stays.*

He does not waltz into our lives over summer break, commune with us a few days, and then retreat to the comfort of heaven, the relationship investment fulfilled. He doesn't show up on a Tuesday night to ladle soup into our bowls, while making sure he keeps the serving counter between us, counting the minutes until he can check another ministry box off his list and get back to the business of life.

God stays.

And if we are serious about reflecting the love of Christ to those in need, we stay. We understand that this is a long-term engagement that demands intentionality in our activity. It is grace with a goal, and that goal is transformative relationships.

I am sitting in my office talking to our student intern, a really godly, thoughtful twenty-year-old. She has just returned from a college mission trip to Taiwan. It clearly was a life-changing experience for her, and I do not want to dampen her zeal or extinguish the fire burning in her eyes. But I do want her to think deeply about what she did and why she did it.

A significant part of her group's time was spent at a shelter for street prostitutes. Each evening, the young women came in from the streets, listened to a sermon, and got a good meal and a safe place to sleep. The college students helped with the meals and did some basic cleaning and picking up in the sleeping area—minimal interaction with those they were serving because of language barriers.

I push her a bit: "You spent a lot of money and invested a lot of time and heart there. What were you trying to accomplish?"

"Mainly just to get God's Word out; they had to listen to a sermon every night before dinner."

"Was there an endgame? Something you wanted to see in their lives? Any long-term provision for them?"

"No, we mainly wanted to let them know they could change, and that God would always be there for them."

Me, gently: "But you were the face of God for them, and you left. You came back to your comfortable life, and those girls are still on the streets every night selling their bodies to strangers. What did you really tell them about God?"

Silence. Thoughtful, reflective silence.

God stays and meets us in precisely the way we most need him to. And as his face and his hands to those who are the outcasts of society, we are called to echo his love to them with extraordinary wisdom. Godly wisdom. An intentional focus on transformation means we act from a position of insight to understand the need. We always engage in a manner that provides the opportunity for transformation.

Remember Lucia who we talked about a few chapters ago? The eleven-year-old selling herself in the slum? Transformation in her life requires relational activity on several levels. Initial crisis intervention means we do essentially whatever it takes to stop the prostitution. Immediately. We talk to her mom, and then, if necessary, to the juvenile authorities. We send the Hope van to her house every day to take her and her siblings to school. We make sure the physical needs of the family are met. We find a way to get her out of the situation.

But rescue does no good if it is a temporary fix. What happens when she is fourteen and much more in charge of her own life? We have a short window of time in which to change the context for her. We put her around boys and girls who have escaped that life, whose own lives have been transformed. We teach her a different way of thinking about herself, about her value as a person rather than as a sexual object. We teach her a trade so she will not be destined to perpetuate the cycles of poverty and despair. We give her hope.

Ultimately, though, it is not just about changing one child's context; it is about redefining a culture. The ultimate answer for Lucia is for her society to reject child prostitution. Millions of girls begin a lifestyle of prostitution without even knowing what they are doing. How do you stop a child from prostituting herself when her community tells her prostitution is a perfectly acceptable means of providing for herself and her family? When she is selling herself before her body has even experienced the changes of adolescence? When she enjoys more approval and appreciation from her abusers than she has ever received at home? When selling herself is just part of growing up?

Childhood prostitution is stopped only by changing a culture, and that is not accomplished in a week-long mission trip. It is accomplished when we consciously and constantly engage for the long run; when our presence becomes a witness for what children can be, rather than how they can be used.

A caveat here. Do not read this as a blanket condemnation of short-term mission trips. They can have an impact, and it can be a very positive one. A while back, our girls' ranch needed two new residences. A mission group from an American church went down to help us with the building process. It was a big group; airfare, hotel, and food probably hit $20,000 pretty easily. They worked hard, long days, hand-digging the pier and beam foundations for one of the new houses. We are talking sunburn-and-bleeding-blisters kind of hard days. At the end of the week they had the excavation for one house ready to go. And then they flew back home with a great sense of accomplishment and personal fulfillment. The next day we hired a backhoe and a drill truck to do the other house. For $500.

But, and this is important, this was not a case of flushing $19,500 to make some American Christians feel good. The youth group kids engaged with our girls, loving them and receiving love. And when they returned home, they were changed. Deeply, profoundly. They told others about us. They gave regularly and led their church to do the same. This was not conscience-salving social tourism. This was mission, in the truest New Testament sense.

The formational question is this: What is the goal? What are we trying to accomplish? Far too often, the answer is to make others look like us, to see them transformed not to the image of Christ, but to our own image. True New Testament ministry always seeks to point others not to our own way of doing things, but to Christ.

A few years ago, a group of young Hope graduates went to our leadership in Brazil. They needed a worshiping and ministering community, but they had discovered that because of their education, their good jobs, their lifestyles, they no longer fit well in the churches of the slums. On the flip side, they really were not comfortable in churches with middle-class membership, either. So they had an idea. If we would help them get started, they would form their own church. And they did. Mind you, this is not Hope's church; it is theirs. And it is an incredible, thriving community of followers. Sure, we helped them get started, and a church from Princeton, New Jersey, worked alongside the graduates to change a dance studio into a worship center, but it's their church.

One of the most profoundly moving experiences of my life came one Saturday night as I watched while former street children—young women who had been trafficked as little girls and young men who had escaped cycles of drug abuse and poverty—were introduced as the leadership team, as the *ministers* of the fellowship.

The really impressive thing, however, is that this is a serving community. They are missional in the truest sense of the word. They host a weekly children's Bible story time for the kids of the abutting slum. They never meet anyone with a destroyed life whom they do not believe God can redeem—because they have experienced that redemption themselves. They are commissioning church planters from their congregation. They are financially supporting the work of Hope through their tithes and offerings. They have become vessels of grace toward others as we were vessels of grace toward them.

The echo of God's love they experienced as children is now resounding in the lives of others.

So act.

Now.

Dirty Faith on Dirt Paths

This isn't a grand social experiment. We don't poke these kids with the needles of our conscience, feed them a bit of gospel along with a bowl of rice, and then leave the rest to nature.

What happens twenty years from now—when they have no family, no future, no hope? Are we satisfied with keeping them alive for another year or two? What's our endgame?

It's clear in the New Testament that Jesus was always looking at the big picture.

"If you knew the gift of God and who it is that asks you for a drink, you would have asked him and he would have given you living water." "Sir," the woman said, "you have nothing to draw with and the well is deep. Where can you get this living water? Are you greater than our father Jacob, who gave us the well and drank from it himself, as did also his sons and his livestock?" Jesus answered, "Everyone who drinks this water will be thirsty again, but whoever drinks the water I give them will never thirst. Indeed, the water I give them will become in them a spring of water welling up to eternal life."[1]

Big picture, long-term view there.

Do we see the big picture, or are we captured by a myopia of the immediate?

I want to know what happens to kids five years out, and I want to know what happens to their eternities. *And*, not *or*. Only when we keep both in focus will we truly be faithful to the New Testament call. Remember last chapter when we talked about crisis intervention? Far too often that is the endgame. We see the dire needs of children in distress, and we apply stopgaps. We feed them, we take them out of brothels, we salve their wounds and perhaps put a bit of ointment on our own guilt. But no long-term fixes—for them or us. Truly caring for the least of these demands transformation, not only of the children in our care but also of our own hearts and our minds.

Cures, not Band-Aids.

One of the most disturbing realities of the abandoned or exploited child crisis is that it is almost always multi-generational. As such, it is self-propagating and constantly growing. Virtually every child who comes to us from the streets or from a situation of abuse is "simply" the most recent in a family lineage of lost children. A prostitute mother has six or eight children for whom street life, abuse, and exploitation are the norm, and then each of those children (or at least the ones who survive) repeat the cycle.

Generation . . . after generation . . . after generation. A geometric progression that ends up with millions upon millions of children trapped in a morass of profound poverty and exploitation.

I cannot tell you how many times I have heard a child, when telling the story of his or her life, say, "I never knew my father, and my mother was a prostitute. . . ." *I was born in the slum, I live in the slum, and I will die in the slum. I don't deserve anything else.* Every story unique, but none is exceptional.

Perhaps the most important task for those of us in orphan work is to break the cycle, not only rescuing the child but changing the trajectory for the generations to come. Our work is not done when the child stops crying from the pain in his belly. Success comes when the subsequent generation—when that child's child—is living a life that is stable, free from abuse and exploitation. Our intersection must be in the very center of the cycle, not a tangential encounter with its edge.

Directional Realities

This is a heart issue—ours and theirs—and it is at the very core of dirty faith. If what we are doing is about us—providing a feel-good rush—then our care will be but a glancing contact rather than the directional care that makes the difference for the homeless, the prostituted child, the teenage prisoner. We will take the quick way out that checks off another box of Christian obligation.

Let me explain it this way. A few years ago, I sat in the office of a real estate developer, talking to him about helping to fund a major project. At the end of the presentation, I asked if he could help. He looked back at me with a thoughtful expression, then a bit of a smile. "This is interesting. You really seem to be on to something good here. So, yes, I will invest, but I am going to give you a choice. I really don't know you well, or know your work. Even so, I will write you a check for $50,000 and in return you will go away and not bother me again. Or you can spend the next several months helping me get to know this project, and, if I decide to buy in, then you will have me for the long term."

Go-away money vs. the investment of heart.

Easy call. That $50,000 was really needed, but still, an easy call. Too often, though, it is not a call we make for ourselves. A long-term investment of our lives, of our hearts, is daunting—a pool deeper than we are comfortable wading. This really is where we need to be leaking grace, echoing God's heart, immersing others in the joy of God's love. *You anoint my head with oil; my cup overflows.*

I want to be careful here. Don't confuse *feelings* with *heart.* Our feelings are never a good indicator of directional reality. Have you ever noticed how Jesus is a really good compass? He is always pointing in the right direction. If north is the direction we need to go, rest assured he is pointing that way. When you look at his interaction with people, he never takes the easy way out, never looks for the panacea that would make them—and him—feel good.

Back to the story of the rich young ruler. I like this guy. I would have accepted a dinner invitation to his house and invited him to mine. And I think Jesus probably liked him, too. At least at first glance, his heart seems to be in the right place—and initially he seems focused on the really important question: *What must I do to get eternal life?*

Mind you, this was not just some question about immortality. This was a heart question. The young man understood that, at its essence, this was a question about what God expected of him. It was the biggest question he could ask. That's why he is talking to Jesus. *And he is trying.* When Jesus hands him a laundry list of the commandments he is to observe, he responds honestly, I think: "All these I have kept." But he knows this is not enough; good heart here. "What do I still lack?" (Matthew 19:20). This is where I want Jesus to let him off, to pat him on the back and say, *"Good job, brother."* I want Jesus to feel for this guy like I do. I want them to hug and everyone to live happily ever after.

But feelings are not a reliable indicator of directional reality. Jesus is in the right place. He acts from an overflowing heart that sees the real need, not from a place of making both himself and the man feel good. Just as with the woman at the well, Jesus sees the big picture here. He tells the young man, "Sell your possessions and give to the poor, and you will have treasure in heaven. Then come, follow me." Matthew records that "when the young man heard this, he went away sad" (Matthew 19:21–22).

Here is the point: Jesus, and we as his witnesses, does not always get to choose the easy way out, the feel-good answer. That's not how overflowing love acts. If our cups are overflowing because of the reality of God's grace in our lives, we will always see the big picture and ask the big question. *We won't settle for a bowl-of-rice-in-a-warehouse answer.*

Too often we give a cursory nod to caring for the least of these. This is hard work—really hard work—that is more than donating our castoffs at the local rescue mission. It's meeting the woman at the well and investing our lives in her eternity. Perhaps it is even digging the well first—and supplying the shovel and the bucket. This is about having our hearts in the right place.

But it is about their hearts, too, and that makes the task extraordinarily more difficult for both us and them. Giving up all his possessions was not just a material issue for the young ruler; it was a spiritual issue, an issue of self-identity. His self-worth, his name, everything was tied up in his possessions. Asking him to give it all away meant that he would be, essentially, giving up himself. Wealth may not be just the cash in the bank. It is, as Jesus says, where our heart is. And that is what transformation requires.

Let me tell the story a different way: a contemporary parable, if you will. *A young child of the streets comes to you and asks, "What must I do to change my life?" And you answer, "You need to be a really good kid; don't lie, don't steal, and don't fight."*

The child answers, "I can do all that and more. I take care of my little brother and sister. What else do I need to do?" And you answer, "I want you to leave the streets, come live with us, and be part of this big family." And the little boy went away sad because he had great freedom on the streets.

Two decades ago, when the doors to Hope's City of Youth first opened, we thought we were prepared. Street kids—dirty, hungry, no one to love them, no future—would have a chance at life. And so the first group of kids came. The team taught them how to shower, gave them new clothes, a bed to sleep in, food, *love*. And as I shared earlier, they all ran away. Not most. All. Every single child.

Freedom was much more important to them than security and love. Independence was their wealth. *And he went away sad because he had great wealth.*

And then Philip, with the help of a local pastor, began to figure it out. Transformation started at the heart level—and that was the most difficult change of all. It meant finding one boy who was ready to walk away from his wealth-identity. And then a second child to be immersed in overflowing grace. Then a third, and there was a core group around which to begin to build a culture. For some of these kids, the education, the warm bed, the vocational training, even the hugs and love were not enough. They needed the transformation of the Father's love. Once their hearts got fixed, we had a chance with everything else.

But here's a different question for you: What if the rich young ruler's answer had been different? What if he had said, "Okay, I'll do this. Now. Today"? Did you notice that Jesus was ready to invest himself in this life? It was not "Sell everything, give it to the poor, and then go do really good things." Nope. It was, "Follow me." Have you ever thought how much more complicated this would have made Jesus' life? He had another man traveling with his little band of brothers, one almost certain to upset the oxcart a bit. This was a rich guy, and Jesus was asking him to travel the countryside, essentially penniless. He was used to people waiting on him, cooking for him. *Ahem, Peter, would you mind toting my satchel for a while? You are much more used to the rugged life than I am.* He was going to fit in really well.

And this was getting pretty late in Jesus' ministry. He had already invested much time in discipling his core group. But he invited another? Was he serious?

Absolutely he was. He understood that asking someone to have their heart transformed means we must be willing to commit our hearts to the journey with them.

God stays.

Dirty faith is always a long-term investment.

Best Intentions and Intentionality

One of the really fascinating things about the ministry of Jesus is that he saw people where they were. He was not a Pollyanna. He knew the rich young man was obsessive about his wealth, the Samaritan woman was a serial bride, and Zacchaeus was a crook. And he knew that the woman caught in adultery really was an adulterer. But he also saw what they could be. More often than not, the path to their future meant they had to come face-to-face with their present, but there was always a path to do so. Not an easy one, but a path. I'll bet Zacchaeus would have loved to hear Jesus say, "Follow me"; it would have gotten him away from the people who despised him. But that was not the way for him. For Zacchaeus to become what he could be, he had to stay right where he was and make restitution to all those he had cheated.

Dirty faith sometimes means dirt paths.

People who are really successful in orphan care see the hard stuff, but they also see the real potential in every child. Honesty time here. I'm probably not there yet. The kids who immediately grab my heart are the poster kids—the ones who are going to end up on the cover of our annual appeal or the first page of our calendar. Or at least the ones who run up yelling "*Tio! Tio!*" when they see me drive up to campus.

My heart still needs some work. But I have been so blessed to watch our staff live out the essence of dirty faith, and perhaps dirtier love. They have a God-blessed grace to look at a twelve-year-old who has been forced to sell her body and see the chaste woman of God she can become. They look at a filthy little thief from the streets and see a leader of men. Remember Adriana and Graziella?

Mas Deus, indeed.

Where we fail in this whole taking-care-of-the-least-of-these business is in a lack of intentionality. When it works, when we track those kids at twenty-five and thirty, when we see them building solid, stable marriages and families, it is always because the hard work was done years and years earlier.

Cures, not Band-Aids.

The programs that work do so because they are less worried about a quick fix than they are about being in it for the long haul. Their goal is never the next hour, the next day, week, or even the next year. Their horizon with the kids is always five, maybe ten years out. It changes the way they do business. Changing the life of a child prostitute is not about getting her off the streets until she is seventeen or eighteen. That is a move, not the endgame. Helping her to have a healthy self-image, knowing she has value beyond that of a sexual object, is a move. Developing vocational and academic skills so she has an alternative to prostitution when she turns eighteen is a move. Not dumping her at the front gate of the shelter when she graduates, but instead providing a year in a transition home where she can learn to live independently is a move.

The endgame is when she stands in front of her church as a self-confident twenty-six-year-old, her husband and two children beside her, and talks about the things God is doing in her life. When her kids are in church and in school. When her marriage is stable. When the cycle is broken. When her eternity is secure. That's the endgame.

Or perhaps, when she becomes the agent of transformation for others.

A little caveat and reminder here—but first a story. The interviewer sat in a chair a few feet away from Philip for a story about Hope Unlimited: "What is the most difficult thing you face in this work?" The question hung in the air several seconds, a cloud passing over Philip's face. He composed himself and began, "For me, the most difficult thing—" He paused, struggling for control again but tears welling up in his eyes. "The most difficult thing is when we invest our lives in a child, and we see the transformation; we see the change. We think this one is going to make it, and then a few months later he runs away to return to the streets, or she graduates and falls back into prostitution. It is absolutely devastating."

Failure.

It happens. We are never promised that our faithfulness will achieve the results we want. It is not always up to us. Remember the parable of the sower? Our responsibility is to see that the seed hits the ground. We can't control what happens after that.

But perhaps the failure is not always what it seems. Back to Philip: "But what I have seen happen time and time again is when one of our former students, who we thought was lost to us forever, approaches us on the street or shows up in church and says, 'When I ran away and went back to the streets, I kept remembering that talk you had with me. I knew the streets were not where I should be.' And they come back, and we see their lives change."

Even with that we know that not all of the kids will make it, that they will not turn out like we hope and pray they will. And so we grieve for them, wanting more for them than they want for themselves. And perhaps grieving drives us to do more, to ask others to join with us, to grasp every opportunity to change the life of a child. And even as we grieve, we rejoice in the fertile soil, the deep, rich soil, and in the seeds that grow to maturity and productivity. There's a lesson here: We are sowers, not soil graders. We cast the seed, do the work without judging the condition of the soil. God gets to know how fertile it is, not us.

What we have to know is this: It's God's game, not ours. Our obligation, our task, our *grace* is faithfulness. And while we are focused on the results, we also have to remember that, ultimately, we do not control outcomes.

I'm sure you're like me. When you see children hurting, you want their pain to go away. You may even want to be an agent of God's grace, but instead, you watch as an indifferent world allows children to languish alone, hurting, without love and hope. Sometimes it's easy to wonder, *Where is God?*

That is especially true when we pour our hearts into children and then watch as they walk away from the love and grace and beauty that God has for them, and return to a destructive life. Where is God?

He is right in the middle of their pain—loving more deeply than humanly possible, more deeply than we can even begin to comprehend. The insight that the psalmist David had into the heart of God simply astounds me. Even as he affirms, "I remain confident of this: I will see the goodness of the Lord in the land of the living," he recognizes that it may not be his timing: "Wait for the Lord; be strong and take heart and wait for the Lord" (Psalm 27:13–14). But catch this: The word David uses for *wait* is the same word meaning "hope." And that is the key to understanding God's provision. He dearly loves and has a plan for each child suffering abuse, abandonment, and neglect in the world. We can wait upon the Lord, because in him we have a certain hope, the promise that he hears the cry of the orphan and will, in his time, bring deliverance.

Again, trust—the very heart of dirty faith.

Ripples

It's a really deep pool, this faith thing. And deep pools create big waves and extraordinary ripples, those waves that break out in concentric circles from the first impact. Something happens when there is true transformation; the waves break out when grace breaks through.

I want you to see the trajectory of the wave here, not just the final breaking on a shore. The pebble of grace is dropped when one person, one Sunday school class, one church, the Church, decides to get serious about New Testament faith. Big-picture faith. *Dirty faith.*

The waves of faith begin to wash over those God has placed in their pool: perhaps a family at a local crisis center, a child adopted into their own home, some street kids in Mozambique, the children of prostitutes in Taiwan, or the kids behind bars in Brazil. Wash over, not lightly splash. Lives and hearts get invested in transformation, and we see directional change in the lives of children.

And the ring of ripples grows.

A few chapters back, I introduced you to The Net Fellowship, a believers' community made up of former children of the street. I do not think I have ever witnessed faith in the power of God to transform lives more evident than it constantly is in this church. It's a place where young adults believe because they have seen. No matter what they encounter, they've seen God fix worse. *"You're an addict living in the weeds of the vacant lot*

COMMUNITY

beside the church? No problem; I spent five years on the street."
"You have been selling your body since you were a teenager?
My mother prostituted me from the time I was eight years old.
God can make you pure again."

And a ripple begins to spread through a Brazilian slum. It quits being okay for a little girl to sell herself. A father chooses to be a part of his family instead of disappearing into the darkness every night. A mother makes sure a little boy is in school and in Sunday school, and his life holds the promise of a future. Because grace causes a ripple in a dirty path.

This fellowship of faith knows the power of God to transform lives, because they have experienced it. They are like Peter and John before the Sanhedrin: "As for us, we cannot help speaking about what we have seen and heard" (Acts 4:20). *They haven't outgrown God.* Perhaps, just perhaps, it's time for us to learn from them, for the waves to wash back on us, if you will. This is what we need to regain: the expectation of God's intervention in the lives of his people.

Dirty faith makes waves.

Corrective Lenses

A Saturday night service at the City of Youth. One hundred fifty or so children who call this place home fill the chapel. Throwaway kids, abandoned, exploited. They all have scars of abuse on the inside; some wear them on the outside.

Prayer time. Gleice walks forward from the back row, takes the microphone from Pastor Derli, and bows her head.

"God, thank you that I am perfect in your eyes."

Yeah.

God, make her perfect in my eyes, too.

Whoever claims to live in him must live as Jesus did.

1 John 2:6

That verse again. The one that says we do not get to redefine faith to reflect our values, that we don't get to baptize the American dream and claim it's New Testament

Christianity. I want to be authentically biblical, and that means seeing people as God sees them. Seeing their need? Of course. Seeing their potential? Absolutely. But, more important, just seeing them. Not identifying them as someone God looks at differently from the way he looks at me.

I want this book to change our world. What author doesn't feel that way about his or her words? I want it to be part of a ball rolling downhill, absolutely crushing the evil in this world that consigns so many people to live on the very fringes of existence. But I want it to change you, too, and that is what this chapter is about. I guess you could call it a devotional chapter. It's time for a bit of soul-searching, of heart examination, helping you—us—get where we need to be. And, ultimately, if enough of us get there, the world is going to change.

Reformation II, anyone?

My first view of Yara was as she sprinted toward a soccer goal and leaped into the air, caught the crossbar, spun her body above the bar, and then let go and balanced on the bar, spread eagle, eight feet off the ground.

Jaw-dropped speechless. And then I heard her story.

Both parents were dead by the time she was seven. She moved into an aunt's home, an aunt who worked as a performer in a circus. Yara was apprenticed by the circus and essentially became a slave. She worked long hours tending animals, learning to perform, had no schooling, ate a subsistence diet of rice and beans, and slept on a mat on the floor. For five years before coming to Hope, she was little more than free labor for the aunt who was to care for her. A throwaway child, not even a blip on the world's radar. Nonexistent.

She is exactly the kind of person our followship of Christ calls us to love—and that means having a relationship and acting upon that relationship. I walk a fine line here, because I really have trouble with this. It is not enough for me to pity Yara, or even to provide for her out of pity. In fact, pity may not solve the problem; it can actually exacerbate it. Pity too often focuses on the separation—the differences—between us. Love, as modeled by Christ and his followers, doesn't see those differences. Living as Jesus did demands relationship with those we are called to serve. Paradoxically, if we are to truly be agents of transformation in the lives of those in need, it can only happen when we no longer find their identity in their need, but when we see them as fellow creations in the image of God, as our brothers and sisters.

That *relationship* word is the hard one. I am absolutely willing and ready to take care of these kids, to make their world better. I will even love them, if you let me define the love.

But—*but*—don't expect me to give up my bedrock conviction that we are not the same. I am an educated American. I deserve my station in life. I'll accept the obligation my position gives me (*noblesse oblige*, indeed!), but *relationship* implies a communing between equals, and I'm not ready for that.

But that is what followship demands, so how do I get there? How do we as Christians really see others as Christ did? How do we not define them in terms of who we are—and who they aren't?

Perhaps we start by learning the difference in identity and circumstance. When we are commanded to take care of the widow and the orphan, when Jesus demands that we give our attention to the least of these—the hungry, the sick, the stranger, the naked, the prisoner—he was not assigning their identity; he was describing their circumstance. *Jesus was fine with who they were; he just did not like their contexts.*

You don't have relationships with circumstances; you have relationships with people.

139

Their identity shows up in the next words: "these brothers and sisters of mine." Understand: We are never asked to change the identity of the least of these; we are asked to change their circumstance.

An important aside here. This is not about people who look and live like me. This is about the others (and then discovering that there are no *others*). Jesus describes it this way in Luke 6:32–35: "If you love those who love you, what credit is that to you? Even sinners love those who love them. And if you do good to those who are good to you, what credit is that to you? Even sinners do that. And if you lend to those from whom you expect repayment, what credit is that to you? Even sinners lend to sinners, expecting to be repaid in full." Then he pushes the envelope: "But love your enemies, do good to them. . . ."

A question for you: What is your image of Jesus? Not Sunday-morning Jesus, but the two-thousand-years-ago-walking-this-earth guy? What did he look like? How did he sound? Did he like the foods you like? *How did he smell?* Would he have fit in with your friends? At your church? Did he have good manners?

. . . the least of these brothers and sisters of mine . . .

Guess who Jesus identified with? Here's a hint: They did not look like you and me. So if I can't recognize the person beyond the circumstance, I need to re-identify Jesus, too. The Lord I talk to in my prayer time is the brother of the filthy kid on the streets of Brazil. His sister is the little girl in the brothel.

Jesus takes it a step further: "Truly I tell you, whatever you did not do for one of the least of these, you did not do for me" (Matthew 25:45). This is not a scorecard where Jesus chalks one up for us every time we do something good for the less fortunate. This is a statement of fact about relationships. *Relationship with others is integral to our relationship with God.* Jesus' indictment is that, if we are not capable of having a relationship with his brothers and sisters, then we do not have a relationship with him. Not a gray judgment here. It's black and white. No relationship with my brothers and sisters in these circumstances, no relationship with me. Determinate, not just indicator.

Listen—this is about your soul here. The very essence of what it means to be Christian is to live in a relationship with God, and Jesus makes it very clear that everyone in relationship with him has to live in relationship with others, and especially, *especially*, with those he called "the least of these." So this is important. Being a follower of Christ is more than believing the right things. *You believe that there is one God. Good! Even the demons believe that—and shudder.* It is more than church attendance or even a daily Bible study and prayer time. It is more than tithing. And it is much more than an annual mission trip. Boiled down to its essence, being a follower of Christ is living in relationship with God and our brothers and sisters.

This is where we need the corrective lenses. It's about seeing, really seeing. So how do we do it? How does Gleice become perfect in my eyes, too? Here's where it starts. It starts when Jesus cures our vision.

One of the healings Jesus performed in the New Testament has always been a bit puzzling because it looks like he didn't get it right the first time. The story goes like this:

> They came to Bethsaida, and some people brought a blind man and begged Jesus to touch him. He took the blind man by the hand and led him outside the village. When he had spit on the man's eyes and put his hands on him, Jesus asked, "Do you see anything?" He looked up and said, "I see people; they look like trees walking around." Once more Jesus put his hands on the man's eyes. Then his eyes were opened, his sight was restored, and he saw everything clearly. Jesus sent him home, saying, "Don't even go into the village."
>
> Mark 8:22–26

141

What just happened here? Did Jesus forget the magic words the first time? Was there a short in the connection?

Nope. We know this was intentional on Jesus' part. So what is the point, what is the lesson embedded in the healing? Look closely at what happened: The blind man saw people, but they were not real to him; they appeared like trees. Objects. Something still needed to be fixed. Seeing people as trees means he's not healed yet. *Once more Jesus put his hands on the man's eyes. Then his eyes were opened, his sight was restored, and he saw everything clearly.* That's a pretty important *then.*

Here's the point, and it's a critical one: Seeing people is a good start, but it is only a partial correction. When people are objects, our vision still needs the healing touch that only Christ can provide.

Let me throw you a curve: In your interaction with them, how do you think the poor, the orphan, the widow see *you?* My guess is they have about as much trouble seeing me as a person, living in relationship with me, looking beyond my circumstance, as I do them. Am I an object to them? Maybe. Do they see me as a spoiled American who has little contact with the reality of existence for the vast majority of the world? Could be. *Probably.* If I cannot see them, their true essential identity, why should I expect them to see me for who I am?

There is a bit of protection in seeing others as objects rather than our brothers and sisters in Christ, especially if the difference in them and us is qualitative rather than quantitative—if the difference is about who they are rather than what they are. We see our stations in life as a result of the efforts we put out, maybe a cursory nod toward blessing, but by and large, we are who we are because of our hard work and brains.

And if we see someone who is not making it, the corollary truth is, well . . .

For most of the world, this self-affirming and back-patting mind-set has little or no basis in reality.

Think about this for a moment. What if there is absolutely no relationship between how hard you work and how things turn out for you? What if your efforts are unrelated to your results? That is the reality faced by millions of the world's peripheral people. They cannot control their economic destiny. They cannot work hard enough or have enough initiative to overcome the hunger in their stomach, or the pained look of hunger in the eyes of their children.

There but for the grace of God . . . We really didn't mean it, but we may have been on to something.

Don't mis-hear me on this point. I am not downplaying the hard work and initiative that got you where you are today. Every successful person I know has put in the time and effort to get there. And the flip side is true, too. There are poor people out there who have made their own bed of poverty. But, for the most part, once you get beyond our border, that is not the way it works. When dealing with the poor, the marginalized, the abandoned, ask yourself, "Could it have played out differently? If the circumstances were flipped—if I had been born the child of a Third World prostitute and Yara had been born into my family—how would things have turned out?"

Keeping the poor at arm's length, treating poverty as an identity rather than a circumstance, allows us to remain comfortable about our station in life.

I have noticed something changing in the American psyche these last few years. As finances have become much more precarious, as we have seen good, hard-working people get the rug jerked from beneath their feet, some of that hubris has begun to disappear. Not quite as smug now. Maybe we have started seeing the possibility for all of us to be that person in need.

Back to our picture of Jesus. How would you judge him if you saw him today? Word chosen intentionally: *judge* him. Because you would, and so would I. But if I am truly to be a follower, I would judge him to be a brother. Here is how John puts it:

> This is how we know what love is: Jesus Christ laid down his life for us. And we ought to lay down our lives for our brothers and sisters. If anyone has material possessions and sees a brother or sister in need but has no pity on them, how can the love of God be in that person? Dear children, let us not love with words or speech but with actions and in truth.
>
> 1 John 3:16–18

The orphan, that widow, this prostituted child are not objects we are rescuing. They are our brothers and sisters whom we are *serving.*

My favorite passage in all of Scripture is in the second chapter of Paul's letter to the Philippians:

> Let each of you look not only to his own interests, but also to the interests of others. Have this mind among yourselves, which is yours in Christ Jesus, who, though he was in the form of God, did not count equality with God a thing to be grasped, but emptied himself, taking the form of a servant, being born in the likeness of men. And being found in human form he humbled himself and became obedient unto death.
>
> vv. 4–8 RSV

What are we to do? Relate to others in precisely the way Christ related to them. And how did he do that? By not claiming the position to which he was entitled, but rather by being a servant.

Don't miss Paul's word picture here: Jesus, who was God, did not demand the prerogatives that were rightly his. Instead, he found it more important to relate to his own creation as a

144

servant. So if God himself is servant, what does that say about the way we ought to be living?

What happens to our world when we as believers see those around us as brothers and sisters to be served? *The corrective lenses of a dirty faith.*

Facing the Reality

I don't like stress. I tend to go out of my way—sometimes to ridiculous extent—to avoid it. I won't watch nail-biter movies or read high-tension novels. I can be a serial confrontation-avoider. That is just my DNA. But I want to cause you some stress right now, because I want you to think about this issue deeply and intentionally. But first a bit of context.

Paul to the Corinthians:

> And now, brothers and sisters, we want you to know about the grace that God has given the Macedonian churches. In the midst of a very severe trial, their overflowing joy and their extreme poverty welled up in rich generosity. . . . Our desire is not that others might be relieved while you are hard pressed, but that there might be equality.
>
> 2 Corinthians 8:1–2, 13

Now for the stress. My brothers and my sisters all over this world are living on the very fringes of existence while I am safe, happy, and prosperous. I don't want to think about them. But I have to.

My brothers and my sisters.

And I am called to be their servant. Can I be content for them to be objects on the periphery of my vision, or will I truly see them as Christ does? Do I claim my rightful place as a privileged American, or do I empty myself of status, become a servant, become obedient? *Have this mind which was in Christ Jesus.*

And then what happens to me? Let's tread carefully here, because what happens to me is really not the issue. If you have read to this point, I am pretty certain you are as disgusted by the purveyors of a health and wealth gospel as I am. Becoming a servant for what we get out of it is as ridiculous as it sounds. Jesus put it this way:

> When you give a luncheon or dinner, do not invite your friends, your brothers or sisters, your relatives, or your rich neighbors; if you do, they may invite you back and so you will be repaid. But when you give a banquet, invite the poor, the crippled, the lame, the blind, and you will be blessed. Although they cannot repay you, you will be repaid at the resurrection of the righteous.
>
> Luke 14:12–14

This isn't silk handkerchief faith; this is long-term investment. But to the question: If I become a servant, how does it play out in my life? The prophet Isaiah gets really serious about justice issues, and he clearly understands the role of the follower of God in making justice happen. Isaiah 58:6–7 again:

> Is not this the kind of fasting I have chosen:
> to loose the chains of injustice
> and untie the cords of the yoke,
> to set the oppressed free and break every yoke?
> Is it not to share your food with the hungry and to pro-
>   vide the poor wanderer with shelter—
> when you see the naked, to clothe them,
> and not to turn away from your own flesh and blood?

But he also understands what happens to the purveyor of justice:

> Then your light will break forth like the dawn, and your
>   healing will quickly appear;

146

> then your righteousness will go before you, and the
> glory of the Lord will be your rear guard.

Isaiah 58:6–8

Do you hear this? Has anyone ever said this about you? One time, just one time, Lord, let someone look at me and say, "The light of his life is like the sun coming up." Just one time.

A close friend joined his church on a mission trip from a small southern town to an eastern metropolitan city. They did the ubiquitous encounter with a different slice of life during their week. While at a rescue shelter, Ken befriended a homeless man over dinner, read Scripture, and prayed with him. Ken's son posted a picture on Facebook captioned, "My dad giving Jesus to a homeless man."

That bothered me. And the more I reflected on it, the more it bothered me. The statement, even at face value, points to the gulf between us: *I have the power and position, and you do not.* I have Jesus; you don't. But, unfortunately, I think it is precisely the perspective we often bring to our interaction with the poor, not just in spiritual matters, but in all things. The giver operates from a position of power and privilege. The recipient, by definition, is the inferior.

I know Ken's son well and also know that there was absolutely no ill-intent in what he was saying, just a poor choice of words from a young teenager. But what if we approach this whole matter differently, where Jesus, or our wealth, or dignity, or security are not something we possess, something to give away, but something we share because we are all recipients of them as gifts from a Father who loves us?

Immediately, how we look at others changes. They quit being *others*. God allows us to see them as he created them. My brothers and sisters. Worth relating to, worth loving.

Love. That word again. We cannot talk about relationships too long before the word *love* rolls into the conversation. It is not just at the heart of our identity. If we have been transformed by the grace of God, it *is* our identity, because it is his identity. God is love.

God is love.

There is no such thing as Christian faith exclusive of love. Faith exudes love, it nurtures love, and it exists only within a matrix of love. Its main mission is to spread love to others, to draw them into its sphere. And love means we cannot see others as objects. Really seeing people means we see them as God does. As John puts it, "If any one says, 'I love God,' and hates his brother, he is a liar; for he who does not love his brother whom he has seen, cannot love God whom he has not seen" (1 John 4:20 RSV). *Once more Jesus put his hands on the man's eyes. Then his eyes were opened, his sight was restored, and he saw everything clearly.*

In a dirty-faith world, Gleice is perfect in my eyes, too.

10

A New Community

"They devoted themselves to the apostles' teaching and to fellowship, to the breaking of bread and to prayer. Everyone was filled with awe at the many wonders and signs performed by the apostles. All the believers were together and had everything in common. They sold property and possessions to give to anyone who had need. Every day they continued to meet together in the temple courts. They broke bread in their homes and ate together with glad and sincere hearts, praising God and enjoying the favor of all the people. And the Lord added to their number daily those who were being saved."

Acts 2:42–47

Now we've gone to meddling. . . .

But this is a tough one. We always hear about the New Testament Church and that it is our model, but we hurry past this section of Scripture and get on to the Corinthian epistles, Philippians, and maybe 1 John—you know, the

149

deeper stuff. And then, when we are really mature, we spend most of our time reading the Revelation of St. John. Part of the problem is that we would much rather talk about theology than about the demands our theology makes on the way we live. Being a-, post-, or premillennialist is a lot more exciting than surrendering our possessions to the Church. And it stays out of our pocketbooks and hearts.

But then we get to that last sentence: "And the Lord added to their number daily those who were being saved."

Why do we want to disconnect the first ninety words from the last thirteen? By any fair reading of this text, we find a cause and effect here—the Lord added to their number specifically because of the way they related to each other, and especially to those in need.

God blessed this stuff, and he uses it to change the world. And if we are serious about those kids in the street, that nine-year-old prostitute, the boy who stares out between the iron bars of his cell—if we are serious about changing the trajectory of their lives, we do it through the community of faith. Important lesson here: The community of faith is not just about the next life; it's about this one, too. When we finally figure out that our commonality in Christ is the matrix for world change, then—then—things will start to happen.

I want to have a conversation with you about community. Not next-door-neighbors community, or even local-church community. Big-picture community. Community in the truest spirit of the New Testament. We use this word a lot as Christians—as the Church (intentionally capital C here)—often with a qualifier like "of faith," and it is important in any discussion of how we live out that faith. So we need to talk about community, how it plays out, how we live it out. But before we get too deeply into this conversation, let's look at a couple of important concepts.

Significance

What makes a life significant? Not the we-are-all-created-in-the-image-of-God kind of significance, but the people-remember-him (or her) level. Perhaps big-S significance. How do you measure it? Almost certainly by impact—positive impact. Will the world be a different place because you were here? Will anyone say, *"For me, Uncle, you are the face of God"*? Will those who observe you from near or afar say, *"The light of her life was like the sun coming up"*? Biblical significance. Here's one for you: How will your obituary read?

Funny thing about obits. The measure of success so many of us cling to in life never appears in our ultimate life story. Think about it. Our society makes it clear that significant people drive really fast cars, have good teeth and great hair, and most important, make a lot of money. But that kind of significance ends at the casket. I've yet to read an obituary that starts out, "He always drove fast cars and had good hair."

Let's put it this way: Obits get it. The final narrative of a person's life usually tells the stories of true significance. The things that made a lasting difference: family, friends, a positive impact in the community . . . and in lives. So how many of us will have an obituary worth writing? Are we significant, or are we more worried about good cars? Are we investing in others, or in possessions? Do we care for the least of these—or for ourselves?

Here is the way Jesus put it: "Do not store up for yourselves treasures on earth, where moths and vermin destroy. . . . But store up for yourselves treasures in heaven. . . . For where your treasure is, there your heart will be also" (Matthew 6:19–21).

151

Interesting concept here: Our ultimate significance in heaven is dependent upon what we find significant here. Read that again: *Our ultimate significance in heaven is dependent upon what we find significant here.* If it is money, position, and power, there will not be much in the way of stored-up treasure. But if we take Jesus seriously about how he wants us to live our lives—if it is about relationships, emptying, *servanthood*—then eternal significance goes off the scale.

As Paul says to the Philippians,

> Many live as enemies of the cross of Christ. Their destiny is destruction, their god is their stomach, and their glory is in their shame. Their mind is set on earthly things. But our citizenship is in heaven. And we eagerly await a Savior from there, the Lord Jesus Christ, who, by the power that enables him to bring everything under his control, will transform our lowly bodies so that they will be like his glorious body.
>
> Philippians 3:18–21

No minced words here; their god is their stomach, and their glory is their shame. Not much gray area. For Paul, being significant was definitional to being a Christian, and significance comes when our minds are set on eternity.

But—and this is one of those important *buts*—don't forget how C. S. Lewis framed this: "If you read history you will find that the Christians who did most for the present world were just those who thought most of the next. . . . It is since Christians have largely ceased to think of the other world that they have become so ineffective in this."[1] The New Testament next-world focus very specifically informed how first-century Christians lived out their lives in relationship both within and beyond the community of faith. Because they saw the big picture, they were significant. And if we were to write their obits two thousand years later, we wouldn't waste much ink on their wealth or

152

popularity. But we might talk quite a bit about the impact they had on the world.

Significance. Isn't that how you want to be remembered?

Now to the next concept.

Stewardship

There is a concept in Scripture that you simply do not find anywhere else in ancient writings. It's called stewardship. Peter puts it this way: "Each of you should use whatever gift you have received to serve others, as faithful stewards of God's grace in its various forms" (1 Peter 4:10). The biblical perspective on possessions is pretty straightforward. As the psalmist says,

> The earth is the Lord's, and everything in it, the world,
>   and all who live in it;
> for he founded it on the seas and established it on the
>   waters.
>
> Psalm 24:1–2

It's God's, not ours, and while he gives us "all things richly to enjoy," the ownership does not change. The fact that it belongs to God changes our relationship with our possessions; we have responsibilities toward them rather than rights emanating from them. Owners have rights, but stewards have responsibilities.

But back to the 1 Peter passage. Did you catch the ultimate object of the stewardship? *God's grace.* That's the big word, the all-encompassing concept. Grace, if I understand the New Testament at all, is how God invests himself in us. It is the giving, not of a discreet substance but of God himself. It is the pouring out of his love, his self-identifying essence, to us. This verse is not just applying to the material, but to everything with which God has blessed us. Paul calls it the treasure in earthen vessels. Knew how to turn a phrase, didn't he?

153

For Peter, it's inclusive. *Every* gift. That means whatever we have—not exclusive to material blessings, but inclusive of the material. *Every* gift.

Then in Acts chapter 2, this is how it plays out: We are in this thing together. Whatever we have, we have for the good of all. When Jesus saw the widow giving her two pennies, he captioned it like this: "Truly I tell you, this poor widow has put more into the treasury than all the others. They all gave out of their wealth; but she, out of her poverty, put in every-thing—all she had to live on" (Mark 12:43–44). And that is what God expects from us.

Look at it this way: God doesn't want our resources; he wants us. Stewardship does not mean giving generous gifts from our possessions. Stewardship means we recognize that they are not ours in the first place; they belong to God. He owns it all. We have been entrusted with his possessions, be they material goods, grace, dignity, freedom. Whatever, they are the blessings, the gifts of God, but they are still his. C. S. Lewis puts it in this context: "Every faculty you have, your power of thinking or of moving your limbs from moment to moment, is given you by God. If you devoted every moment of your whole life exclusively to His service, you could not give Him anything that was not in a sense His already."[2] Inclusive. Every gift.

Do you want to radically experience the presence of God in your life? Start living biblically; start living as if your life is not you own, as if it all belongs to God. "They broke bread in their homes and ate together with glad and sincere hearts, praising God and enjoying the favor of all the people. And the Lord added to their number daily those who were being saved" (Acts 2:46–47). That's what God blesses.

Important point: All the language in Scripture about what God expects out of us, and then what he will do for us, was not—is not—an abstraction.

Give generously to them and do so without a grudging heart;
then because of this the Lord your God will bless you in all your
work and in everything you put your hand to.

Deuteronomy 15:10

None of this is a hypothetical. It was proven in the labora-
tory of the church of Jerusalem. The first Christians got really,
really serious about community. They took God's words—his
expectations—at face value, and it proved out for them. They
discovered God was serious, too; he meant it when he described
a lifestyle he would bless. *We did this, and here was the result.*
Reality, not abstract musings.

So how do we handle this? Is this really what New Testament
faith looks like? What does God really expect here, and what
will he bless? Or perhaps, how dirty are we ready for our faith
to be? I am not going to insist here that the Jerusalem church
is our model for its structure and organization (although that
shouldn't be rejected out of hand), but it certainly and absolutely
is the model in terms of obedience, commitment, community,
and probably most important, radical trust in God's provision.
The question for the modern church is quite simple: *Can we
exist as a community faithful to the teachings of our Lord when
the wealth of the Church is concentrated in the hands of so
few, and so many believers survive on the margins of existence?*

If the answer is no—and it has to be—then how do we get
there from here? How do we start living like Jesus lived?

Perhaps the starting point is a re-understanding of what it
means to be Christian and what it means to be Church. Not a
new understanding, but a return to the orthopraxy of the New
Testament. And perhaps as we do this we'll care for the widow,
the orphan, the sick, the stranger, and the prisoner. And our
Lord will say, "You have done it unto me."

So to the whole idea of community—but, again, a circuitous
path to get there . . .

Have you ever thought about what it was like to be a first-century Christian? To be a fellowship of believers before "church" was even a concept? No real guidebook. Sure, they had the Old Testament, but the new wineskins paradigm made it clear that the covenant community was going to be different from what was already extant. Not exactly a blank slate in front of them, but they were going to have to figure it out.

I really want you to get this picture. One of the recurring descriptions of the first Christians is that they were an alien people, sojourners, strangers. Perhaps another way of saying it is that they were "a people out of time." They weren't like the folks around them. The New Testament Church was an anticipatory community—a group of people living out life not as it is, but as it is to be in heaven. In a very real sense, they were living the presence of the future.

Perhaps the clearest evidence of the reality of the Holy Spirit in the lives of the first followers of Christ is that the Church did not implode upon itself. Think about this: They were horribly estranged from their families, their synagogues; they were seen as heretics; they were soon persecuted. And then they were asked to embrace a way of living that was as concerned about the needs of those around them as it was about their own needs. But they prospered. Maybe not materially, but as community.

What we get in the first chapters of Acts is Christianity stripped to its essence. There is no organizational structure developed in the Church yet. The detailed doctrines of grace and Christology we find in Paul's letters are decades away. John's eschatology is not even on the horizon. So what we see in the Jerusalem church is the most basic understanding of what it means to be a community of Christ followers. This is not layered Christianity; this is the foundation. And what is important to them? Focusing on God—*They devoted themselves to the apostles' teaching . . . and to prayer.* And focusing on each other—*They devoted themselves . . . to the breaking of bread . . . and to fellowship. All the believers were together and had everything in common. They sold property and possessions to give to anyone who had need.*

Again, picture the community: isolated, persecuted, impoverished. But look how they lived: *with glad and sincere hearts, praising God.* They were not keeping score the way the rest of the world was.

The central feature of everything they were and everything they did was community. The very first description we get of what it means to be Christian is community. Do we understand that today? I'm not sure we do.

Almost five hundred years ago, Luther discovered what he called "the strange new world of the bible," and launched the Protestant Reformation. At the heart of this movement was the conviction that Christian faith is not about structure, organization, and transaction, but about relationship, and that conviction has repercussion for both who we are and how we live. The central fact of our existence is our relationship with Jesus Christ, and this relationship informs and drives our relationships with all others. Peter describes it this way: "Having purified your souls by your obedience to the truth for a sincere love of the brethren, love one another earnestly from the heart" (1 Peter 1:22 RSV). The writer of Hebrews says, "Let brotherly love continue" (Hebrews 13:1 RSV). The love Christians are to have for each other flows from the relationship with Christ and bears his special mark. Here is the important piece: community is a type of relationship rather than a structure.

Brotherhood in Jesus Christ—not friendship, not proximity, not common interest, and not even personal intimacy—was the foundation of the community in the New Testament. And when you get beyond the first chapters of Acts, you find these communities springing up throughout the New Testament world—in

157

Galatia, in Ephesus, in Corinth, in Smyrna—where the Jerusalem model was replicated over and over again. Community meant a total commitment to those who shared faith in Jesus Christ, even those beyond the sphere of immediate contact, even with people they did not know at all. So Paul could write to the Corinthians about the believers in Macedonia, "Our desire is not that others might be relieved while you are hard pressed, but that there might be equality" (2 Corinthians 8:13). The community acted in concert. *We are all in this together, and together we have the resources to make things right.*

That is a lot of build-up, but there is a point. Those kids in Brazil, that child prostitute in eastern Europe, the twelve-year-old soldier in Africa are all part of this community, too, and I am absolutely responsible for where they end up in this world and the next. My community is big enough to take care of them.

I'll be honest with you. My impulse is to draw the circle of community as tightly as I can. I want it to be people who look like me and sound like me, or, at the very least, live close enough that I can occasionally rub elbows with them. But that's not biblical. It was not the way the first Christians understood community, and it certainly wasn't the way Jesus described it.

> But he wanted to justify himself, so he asked Jesus, "And who is my neighbor?" In reply Jesus said: "A man was going down from Jerusalem to Jericho, when he was attacked by robbers. They stripped him of his clothes, beat him and went away, leaving him half dead. A priest happened to be going down the same road, and when he saw the man, he passed by on the other side. So too, a Levite, when he came to the place and saw him, passed by on the other side. But a Samaritan, as he traveled, came where the man was; and when he saw him, he took pity on him. He went to him and bandaged his wounds, pouring on oil and wine. Then he put the man on his own donkey, brought him to an inn and took care of him. The next day he took out two denarii and gave them to the innkeeper. 'Look after him,' he said, 'and

158

when I return, I will reimburse you for any extra expense you may have.' Which of these three do you think was a neighbor to the man who fell into the hands of robbers?" The expert in the law replied, "The one who had mercy on him."

Jesus told him, "Go and do likewise."

Luke 10:29–37

Jesus never describes community geographically or demographically; he always describes it actively. Community is defined by activity. So here is the point of all this. Those 153 million orphans, the uncounted millions of sex-trafficked children, the 1.1 million kids in prison? We impact them when we take community seriously. When the Church is a force in the world. When we roll up our sleeves and make a difference for these children. When we practice dirty faith.

We can do this. Jesus did not commission us for inactivity. Jesus to Peter: "And I tell you that you are Peter, and on this rock I will build my church, and the gates of Hades will not overcome it" (Matthew 16:18). That's not a description of a defensive position. This is a picture of the Church that is absolutely a battering ram against the evil in this world, an evil that assigns people to the periphery of existence, an evil that says it's okay for a mother to sell the body of her ten-year-old daughter, an evil that corrupts the soul of the Church with materialism and selfishness. We are commissioned to destroy this evil.

We can make the difference; we have been blessed with stewardship of the resources. From chapter 3: *If Christians chose to give 10 percent of their income, and churches chose to devote 60 percent of that increased giving to "least of these" needs, there would be $98.4 billion available for changing the context internationally with an additional $32.8 billion for domestic missions. And, by the way, as we meet those needs, we also gain the moral and spiritual stature to share with the world the good news that Jesus loves them and died to bring them eternal life.*

Again, Paul gets it right: "Our desire is not that others might be relieved while you are hard pressed, but that there might be equality" (2 Corinthians 8:13). We are not talking about sacrificial giving here. We're talking about minimal tithing and getting serious about seeing Jesus' brothers and sisters as part of our community.

But a critically important reminder: This isn't just about our checkbooks; this is about our lives. This is about immersing ourselves in obedience. About embracing those the world has discarded. Living, engaging, *loving* the brothers and sisters of Christ. *My cup overflows,* and often on a dirty path.

We can do this, because, even more important, we have been entrusted with the spiritual authority to face this evil and absolutely destroy it. If you really want to get a picture of who we are in the world, read the letters of John. By the time he writes them, he's an old man; he has seen all the evil this world has to offer—and it was plenty. But still—*still*—you see that extraordinary assurance of the sufficiency of grace and God's provision: "You, dear children, are from God and have overcome them, because the one who is in you is greater than the one who is in the world" (1 John 4:4).

At its essence, this is a spiritual battle played out in the very material realm, and it must be engaged on both fronts. When our hearts are right, when we live in community, when we see the least of these as our brothers and our sisters, then our lights rise in the world.

A couple of years ago an absolutely stellar young man was finishing his time at our City of Youth, preparing to move to our graduate transition house. He was thrilled to be graduating, but he had a weight on his heart. When the authorities had brought him to Hope, Alexandro had left a brother, Calebe, on the streets of São Paulo. As far as he knew, Calebe was still alive, still on the streets. Over the years, our staff had made inquiries, trying to find Calebe, but finding one child among the city's tens of thousands of kids was a long shot. But Alexandro pleaded with our social workers: Could we try one more time? So one more trip was made to the old neighborhood in São Paulo, asking if anyone knew of a street boy named Calebe who had a brother named Alexandro. And the unimaginable happened: Calebe was found. Hungry, dirty, homeless, but alive. Our staff sat down on the sidewalk with him, explained that Alexandro had been at a place called Hope, told him about his brother's new life. Tears began streaming down Calebe's face. "For the love of God, can Mr. Hope help me, too?"

Yes, Calebe, he can. For the love of God.

This is dirty faith.

Lives of Dirty Faith

Consistent theme here: There are no super-Christians. A super-faith has never been what God expects of us. Take a look at Hebrews chapter 11, where the writer lists our pedigree of faith. Abraham was such a coward that he refused to acknowledge Sarah was his wife, Moses murdered and ran, Rahab was a prostitute, David an adulterous murderer. But these folks define what it means to be the faithful?

Yep. Good enough definition for me. God understands our weakness, but frailty is never an excuse for inactivity. In spite of—in the midst of—weakness and brokenness, we can still be used of God.

> Religion that God our Father accepts as pure and faultless is this: to look after orphans and widows in their distress and to keep oneself from being polluted by the world.
>
> James 1:27

Normative, acceptable faith. Expected religion.

So what now? Sell our belongings, head to Brazil, Africa, Thailand, or at least southern Appalachia? Live out our lives on the streets of Bangkok, or perhaps in a village near Maputo? Perhaps, but probably not. I know that is not the answer today for me and my family, and not for most of you, either. But we have to take this thing seriously. We really have to engage at a deeper level. A generic stirring of the emotions is not enough. While we are sitting here feeling a real burden in our hearts for the cast-off children of this world, tens of thousands are dying; million are hurting, hopeless.

Faith without works is dead.

James 2:20 NKJV

So act. Now. *But how? Where?*

Fortunately, there are guideposts on this path of dirty faith; not super-Christians, but some folks who have figured it out—or are at least far enough down the path in the journey to guide the rest of us. They are pathfinders, but truly followers—practitioners of dirty faith in the deepest sense of the phrase. They are living lives of profound faith and profound impact, and you find them living this out in everyday places. I want you to know a few of their stories: people, churches, communities I have encountered while walking down this dirty path. None of them were rising superstars on the American evangelical scene when they were overwhelmed by God's grace and it began to spill over on the tertiary people, the orphan, the child prostitute, the kid lost in the system. Just followers, being faithful to the love of God they experienced in their own lives. In many cases, you will hear their stories in their own voices.

This is dirty faith, and these are its practitioners.

Before we launch into the stories of people who are living dirty faith, I want to tell you a different story for context— a backstory, if you will. One of the most amazing things about our God is how absolutely unimpressed he is by human-imposed power structures, how God of the Powerless so often chooses to do his work through the powerless. How the outcasts, the ones declared extraneous by the world, become the center of his kingdom. *Lazarus, the one God helped.* Revival, renewal, Reformation rarely begin in the seats of power. The hand of God moves in places of humility, in quiet obedience. A sea change is rising in the way the Church looks at orphans—and it started in a small church in Africa.

A few years ago, Zambian pastor Billy Chondwe looked around his community and saw the impact of AIDS and poverty. Compelled by his understanding of Scripture's call to care for the widow and the orphan, Billy passionately called his church to meet the needs of the orphans in his local community. An American visitor watched as church members began to step forward and give—not out of their abundance, but out of their poverty—to care for the orphans. One woman gave the shoes off her feet. The American, Gary Schneider, president of Every Orphan's Hope, was so moved that he began to help Zambian leaders coordinate Orphan Sunday efforts across the country. What began that day as a plea for obedience grew into a movement, first in churches in Zambia and Africa, and then to the U.S.[1] Today, Orphan Sunday is a worldwide movement that expresses exactly who we are as the Church. And it began not because an internationally famous Christian leader picked up the cause, or because a high-profile church decided to get involved, but because a small village pastor saw the need around him and believed it is every Christian's calling to respond.

Not super-Christianity; normative Christianity.

And now for the stories of serious followers. . . .

Compassion on the Periphery

Dr. Burt and Mimi McDowell didn't become believers until they were in their forties, but they've lost no time learning—and following—the commands of Christ. Today, in their sixties and recently retired, the McDowells do not let their involvement with Hope Unlimited for Children suffice as doing for the least of these. In addition, they spend one day each week seeing patients at the Samaritan House free clinic for underserved families. They minister to the working poor, sharing God's love with those who have been pushed to the margins of life. Dr. McDowell contrasted the clinic with his years of working as a doctor in a traditional setting: "At the clinic, there is no hierarchy. It's an egalitarian community. We get to serve the most wonderful, humble patients. It's truly beautiful."

When not working at the clinic, both Burt and Mimi are committed to mentoring—he through marriage mentoring ("It's like a vaccine for marriages") and she through helping women become liberated from the guilt and shame of their pasts by offering them biblical hope and introducing them to God's love. *Even people we would never suspect find themselves lonely on the periphery.*

The couple understands that, whether working with people of poverty or affluence, the realities of life are often messy. Many times, the only answer is to love people right where they are, letting the treasure of love God placed in each of them overflow and redeem everyone it touches. The McDowells have learned the lesson well: Redeeming others is part of our own redemption.

Godly Eyes

It is not always an easy path; in fact, it is almost always a difficult one. But the journey begins not with our feet, but with our eyes. It begins when we start looking for the moments of grace in the lives of others. And so I want you to hear a story of seeing through the words of the seer, Lynn Staley.

Chuck and I were married in 1971, but we were not able to have children. Seventeen years later, in 1988, a pastor from a local church called us because he had a pregnant mother who was looking for a Christian home for her unborn baby.

On May 7, 1988, David was delivered by a family friend who was a local physician.

Three days later, on May 10, our senior pastor and his wife joined us at the hospital as the nurse introduced us to our new baby boy. That is when I saw the heavens open and the hands of God hand me my son—the answer to seventeen years of prayers.

David was a gift from God and fit our family perfectly. His sweet spirit and quick wit always made us laugh and filled our home with joy. He always knew how to diffuse a tense situation—whether at home or at school—with humor. Everyone he met was a friend; classmates told us, "He liked everybody!"

In 1991, God blessed us with Catherine Lynn. She was a miracle baby the doctors never expected. She was indeed God's second gift to us. In every single family picture, David has his arm around his little sister; he was her protector. They were best buddies.

Fast forward to Monday, Labor Day, September 3, 2001. David was thirteen. Around five o'clock in the evening, he was crossing the country road in front of our neighborhood on his moped. A car, driven by the son of friends of ours, was coming at 70-plus miles per hour. David wasn't accustomed to judging that much speed, so he crossed the road—but there wasn't time. He was taken by ambulance to Community Hospital in Anderson, and then by Lifeline to Methodist Hospital, Indianapolis.

He died around eight o'clock. Had he lived, he would have been paralyzed from the chest down.

The next day, Tuesday, after a long night of shock and grief, we invited the teenage driver and his parents to our home. As difficult as it was, we could not escape the thought that Jesus had forgiven us of so much; how could we in turn not extend that same forgiveness we had received to this young man?

He entered our foyer. I hugged him. We sobbed together. As I held him close, I whispered in his ear, "We forgive you. It was an accident. David is with Jesus. He is ok."

The presence of the Holy Spirit in our home that morning was unmistakable. . . .

At the funeral on Friday, our church sanctuary was filled with family and friends who offered their support and prayers. We invited the young man and his parents to join us in the section of the church reserved for family. We didn't want him to be ostracized, excluded, or rejected.

I needed to return to teaching at Ball State University that Monday, only one week from the accident. I couldn't even begin to think about teaching. My brain was like mush.

Then the young man's mother offered to pray for me— and God anointed her to pray me through my teaching. She wrote a personal note of encouragement and prayer and Scripture every single week for over two years. I still have them.

God gave her specific Scriptures just for me—just what I needed—just for that week. God used her to help me move on. I could only take it one day at a time.

Forgiveness was the step I had to take first in order for God to heal my broken heart.

I returned to class the very next week on the morning of 9/11. We watched the television in my classroom as I ministered God's peace to my frantic students. God knew I needed to be there. The very next weekend, I chaired the Early Childhood Conference for Ball State University. God was faithful in 1988 when David was born, and God was faithful in 2001 when David died. God was faithful to sustain us then, and God continues to be faithful to us now. We have learned that we can depend on him.

This, friends, is the very essence of what it means to be a follower of Christ. Extending grace in the middle of our brokenness, our pain. Cups overflowing in the presence of a loving, holy God, soaking the world around us with his grace.

Sojourning Toward Biblical Hospitality

It's a journey, this dirty faith thing. And we trust God that more and more sojourners are called to travel this path. Take David Anderson, for example, a quiet, unassuming man not afraid to ask questions. As a teenager, he asked himself how he could afford college. The answer was to follow in his father's footsteps, working as a bricklayer while attending school.

And then that first telling step onto the path of dirty faith. After graduating and getting married, he and his wife, Karen, became houseparents in a group home for twelve troubled teens. It was his first experience with children whose life paths were less than ideal, so another question: *Is there something more I can do for children like these?* He then followed the path of his pastor/seminary professor/grandfather, attending Trinity

Divinity School in Chicago and eventually earning a doctorate in clinical psychology with a focus on children.

He opened a clinic, spending the first half of his career dealing with the victim side of child abuse—evaluating children, documenting their stories, prosecuting their parents. He and Karen became foster parents, and the stories became personal.

Dr. Anderson began looking at the situations of the parents, asking himself what effect they had on the children. Stressful lives, situations out of hand, abused children, but no venue for early intervention. Children were protected only *after* the fact of abuse. And so, more questions: Why do parents abuse their children? The answer in the vast majority of cases involved a lack of support, social isolation, no caring neighbors. Is prior intervention possible? What can the Church do—again, as in the past—to make a difference?

Dr. Anderson became a pastor, increasingly convicted that the Church was losing its place in society as a significant social change agent. While serving as executive director of Lydia Home, he encountered mothers who needed help, but Lydia Home couldn't help in situations where no abuse was present, so he and Karen became the hands of God in those situations *before* the fact—and the spark of hope that would become Safe Families for Children was struck.

With a handful of volunteers lined up, Dr. Anderson sent a letter to Chicago mayor Richard Daly, outlining his idea for how Christians would take in children when their parents needed temporary help; how they would provide a "reset button" for stressed parents before abuse entered the picture, before a loving but overwrought parent lost custody. To his surprise, the mayor responded with seed money, allowing about a half-dozen families to be served.

Dr. Anderson got it: Biblical hospitality was the answer to the questions he'd been asking for so long. So he moved forward, scheduling a meeting with a key person in child welfare, hoping to get his blessing. Instead, he was told, "It will never work; don't waste your time." And hear the rationale, because this is the way the world sees us—often with very good reason: (1) Christians only protest things; they don't do anything proactive, and (2) Children are not valuable in our society unless they're your own or you adopt them.

Cultural irrelevancy, perhaps?

While Dr. Anderson chose to disprove the man's first reason, he says the second one—the "ownership issue"—is the greatest uphill battle he faces. Loving and sacrificing for children not their own (either by DNA or adoption) is a challenge for people, but as he heard a conference speaker say, "We've got to get over our hang-up with DNA. If we truly love children, we will love their parents."

The calling of Safe Families is to love children as if they were our own—but for a short period of time. Just as healthy churches take care of their own *and* reach out to others, healthy families do, too.

And God not only approves, he blesses. The quest for "healthy families" is catching on. In Chicago alone, there are now 920 host families who care for nearly one thousand children. Sixty-five cities in the U.S., U.K., Canada, and Kenya are resurrecting the ancient, biblical "love of strangers," impacting their communities by traveling this path of faith, caring short-term for children while a parent gets needed help; keeping families together and children out of "the system"; offering long-term success without the scars of abuse.

This is not a business-as-usual approach to children and families in trouble. This practice of biblical hospitality is a radical departure from our existing child welfare system, but it is changing lives, and it offers the Church the chance to be *the* answer to many of society's current problems. The questions Dr. Anderson asks today are: Who will be the next host family, Safe Family church, Safe Family friend? Who will practice dirty faith?

New Testament Community

What happens when believers become followers, when the Church starts to act like the body of Christ? What happens when we take the words of the New Testament seriously, when we affirm by our activity that religion that is pure and undefiled before God and the Father is this: *to look after orphans . . . in their distress and to keep oneself from being polluted by the world?* The answer may look a lot like Project 1.27.

In 2004, pastor Robert Gelinas of Colorado Community Church confronted some disturbing numbers, especially when seen in juxtaposition: 875 kids, legally available to be adopted, were languishing in the state foster care system. And three thousand churches in Colorado were by and large unengaged with the need.

Anyone see the disconnect here?

In fact, pastor Gelinas knew there were enough churches in the Denver area alone for all those kids to have homes. He looked at the need and knew: Simple obedience would change the trajectory for hundreds of children. As he said then, "The body of Christ needs to come together to make sure there are no children waiting for homes in Colorado. It is a travesty that we have kids waiting for homes in our own backyards. That should never be the case. . . ."

And so he started conversations with friends and church leadership—and Project 1.27 found life.

James 1:27: Religion that God our Father accepts as pure and faultless is this: to look after orphans . . . in their distress.

Essential dirty faith.

They knew the statistics for foster kids: Something over half of the boys who age out of the foster care system end up incarcerated—in most cases within two years. As high as 75 percent of sex traffic victims have a history in foster care.

Speaking up for the kids is not just something the Church can or might do, it is the very essence of our identity.

So the work began: recruiting and training families, working with state and county officials to meet statutory requirements, educating them about how Christian faith needs to be incorporated into the system. In a very real sense, re-envisioning what it means to be Church. But it also meant helping local churches understand what it means to care for these children—and how it is our common task, the calling for each of us who claim to be followers. Shelly Radic, president of Project 1.27, says, "Foster and adoptive families are far too often seen by outsiders as super-parents. When things go wrong, as they always will, many foster parents feel that they can't ask for help because they are supposed to be super-parents. Instead, what the Church has to do is develop believers who understand that being a foster parent is a 24/7 job—and then be there to offer support."

What Project 1.27 is doing is not an add-on ministry; it is central to what it means to be the Church. As someone standing outside looking in, I would describe the message of Project 1.27 this way: These kids are a part of our family, and we are all in this thing together. Acts 2 kind of together. And that togetherness is what can make the difference. Throughout the twentieth century, churches have been increasingly committed—and successful—to inspiring families to foster or adopt children, but they haven't been overly interested in being there for those families in the long-term.

That's not how it works in Project 1.27. Every fostering or adopting family candidate brings at least four individuals or families into the process with them. This is their support team, providing them encouragement, relief, an extra pair of

hands. Perhaps one member of the support group is research-
ing how to address special educational needs of a foster child;
another is providing a once-a-week respite for the parents;
maybe someone else is on emergency call; someone mows the
grass. Not profound acts, but profound differences in the life
of a family and in the future of a child. The Church—living
as a community of faith.

How does it play out long-term? Working with the churches
and with state and county agencies, the 875 children originally
waiting to be placed have been reduced to less than three hundred. Over five hundred Christian families have opened their
homes to children once trapped in the system; 248 of them have
been adopted.

This is the kind of difference we are called to make for cast-
off children.

Traffic

It's not just Thailand or eastern Europe. Modern-day slaves are
here, on our streets, in our communities. And Alene Snodgrass[2]
knows them. You need to hear her voice:

> In the past few years, while loving on others in the darkest
> of places, I've witnessed trafficking. Women being bought
> and sold for a price against their will. I've walked into
> clubs to love on girls and shine Jesus' light only to hear
> the stories that they were forced there by their boyfriends
> or dads. They were not free to leave until they had earned
> their money. I've served on the streets and met the girls
> who were being forced to sell their bodies so that others
> could have drug money.
>
> Everywhere I looked my heart broke at such a deep
> level. I was devastated as I heard the cries of these girls

and yet had no help to offer. Sometimes saying "I'll be praying for you" seems so lame when you know the girl is crying for someone to rescue her. My soul was sad as I had realized how many years I spent in a clueless world—not knowing, not caring, not believing.

Slavery still exists! It's not only happening in Asia, it's happening in your city, too. Because I live so close to the Mexico border, many here think trafficking only deals with those who are "trafficked" here from another country. This is not so. It is any person—man or woman—who is enslaved in any way domestically or internationally. The women I mentioned above are being trafficked—sold!

I can't escape it.

The more I learn, the more angered I become. While we sit in our comfortable homes and churches, there are people out there being bought and sold. Modern-day slavery at its finest.

It's so much easier to be clueless. I've done that for the majority of my life. Oh, how I can tell you, it's a happy place. Clueless, comfortable, and self-centered—that was me. While I call it a happy place, it really wasn't. There was an emptiness deep within my soul because that is not the way God created us to live. With the announcement that my church, Bay Area Fellowship, would be opening a Rescue House came a whole new level of awareness for me. God will not let up.

I've visited with a woman who was bought and sold to others by her grandfather.

I've sat across the table in meetings from those in authority within our city and told the stories and said, "YES, this is happening in our town!"

I've gone away for a weekend looking to escape the burden my heart feels only to meet another soul who was

trafficked from a northern state deep into the woods of
Mexico and held against her will for years.

God is nudging us to wake up!

I truly believe this. I think he is sickened that we have
convinced ourselves that putting on our pretty dresses and
attending a suburban church on Sunday is what classifies
us as Christian. Have you read the Bible recently? Have
you followed Jesus and his story? Nowhere do I see this as
the example laid out before us. Nowhere!

Please don't think for a minute that I have this all figured out—I don't. I feel like a sleepy Christian who is just
waking up from a long hibernation of truth. I'm clumsy
and just as afraid of the next step as you are. But one thing
I know. God woke me up to the burdens of his heart, and
for that I'm thankful!

Focus

Who needs to hear that Jesus loves them? Who needs the hands
of Christian care extended to them? We all do, of course. But it
is so much easier to "minister" to those who look like us, who
do not move us from our comfortable complacency. But that's
not biblical, and it is certainly not Christlike.

Ministry focus was a choice Calvary Chapel of Ft. Lauderdale,
Florida, had to make a few years ago. Plans were underway at
the church to develop a new Christian school for the children
in the church and surrounding community. A needed ministry?
Absolutely.

But reality kept interjecting itself into the life of the church.
As family pastor Doug Sauder explained, "We were seeing the
headlines every day: foster children; missing, abused, and abandoned children. An overcrowded system absolutely broken. And

the people in our church kept putting these headlines in front of our staff. They just would not go away."

So the senior pastor cast a compelling vision for the church. What was the greatest community need: a school for the children of church members and others in the community who were a lot like them, or providing homes for children who had none? The Christian school really was a great project, but it wasn't on the order of taking care of kids with no place to live.

And so 4KIDS of South Florida was born. *This* is what it means to be Church.

Today, 4KIDS provides homes for over two hundred children all along the continuum of care: foster homes, an intake center, a crisis pregnancy home. And twenty to thirty children each year are adopted into new families.

The echo of God's love.

And in this, relevancy happens. Sauder estimates that 15 to 20 percent of church members are involved in caring for these children. Somewhere around 30 percent of the pastoral staff are adoptive or foster parents. As president of 4KIDS, Sauder sees more than just the impact on the children; he sees what it does to the church. "There is no question that this ministry has added depth to the DNA of the church," he says. "Foster child ministry is one of the most difficult ministries a church can start because the foster family gets wrapped into the difficult realities of raising children who bring problems into the home with them. Confronting these realities brings a new depth to our families—and then to the church itself."

And when the church began to see others in a different light, when foster parents brought biological parents to church with them, when the "haves" started standing side by side with those who do not have, the fabric of the church itself began to change.

Relevance. The community now sees the church in a different light. The energy, the passion for vulnerable children, resonates beyond its walls. The willingness to tackle the problem of kids who are really hurting speaks to those who had written the church off as largely irrelevant to their lives. And other churches began to see the pattern. They saw the hurt and pain around us, extended the love of Christ to those in need, and "God added daily to their number." Now, over two hundred churches are engaged with the work of 4KIDS.

I will say it again: This is not easy work, this caring for the least of these. It can stretch us far, far beyond our zone of comfort. But it is absolutely necessary. Hurting children, kids exploited, abandoned, consigned as peripheral to all the world's concern, are not only on the streets of Brazil, or in a prison in the Sudan, or in a brothel in Calcutta. They are there, to be sure, but they are all around us. God may want you on some dirt path in the Third World, but then again, he may just want you to look down your street. We're in this thing together.

So let's act now.

Essentials

Longer story here, but I want you to hear it. Perhaps I should have just made this chapter 1, and then the book could have been a lot shorter.

I really wish this book had photos, because when I first saw the photo of Cory and Shannan[3] Martin's family, I thought, *That's it. That is what dirty faith looks like.* The gene pool represented in their children is pretty wide and deep, and their family tree is more of a small forest.

I am not quite sure how to tell their story because the painting of their lives changes like one of those holographic cards—it really does depend on your angle. But in every facet, there is a deep and reflective pool of overflowing grace. This is relevance.

Cory is the chaplain at the Elkhart County, Indiana, jail, and Shannan is a stay-at-home mom and writer. Beyond the two parents, there are Calvin and Silas from Korea, and Ruby—American-born with roots in Malawi. And not long ago, the Martins unofficially adopted a nineteen-year-old young man who comes from a difficult past.

Shannan describes their journey to adoption this way:

What I know now is that God simply had a different family in mind for me. He knew all along that my boys would have almond eyes and my daughter would have the regal forehead of an African queen. He knew that our oldest son would find us late in life and make us believe he had always been right here. It was no surprise to him. God put us together in such an amazing way, he plucked us up and tied us together, knowing how each piece would complete the puzzle.

God is right in the middle of this story.

The Martins' oldest son was recently released from prison, but while making weekly visits to see him, they were impacted in another way—one of those ripples of expanding grace. As Cory describes it, "Through knowing him we got to know someone else in the jail. We started visiting this woman and corresponding with her, and we realized that for a lot of inmates, we were the only contact they had with people on the outside. They're dying to have someone they can talk to that will talk with them, be friends with them, and treat them like a normal person." The relationships formed there led to a new conviction, a new calling, and then a career change: Cory became chaplain for the county jail. Maybe Jesus was serious when he said, "I was sick and in prison and you visited me." Remember: Deliverance, not just appearance.

But there is another part to this sojourn, a truly dirty path, and its end is nowhere in sight. When I first heard it, I thought,

This is exactly what I am talking about—the very definition of life among the least of these. And then I wondered why this is not the norm, why this is not the way we are all living out our faith. The Martins lived on a wonderful farm in rural northern Indiana, a postcard place to raise their expanding family. But God nudged. Maybe the isolation, the *protection*, of the farm wasn't what he wanted for them. Shannan and Cory both got to the same conclusion at the same time: God was asking them to sell their farm. They had both begun to realize how it kept them secluded from their neighbors—next door and across the ocean. Shannan explained, "Before we knew what was happening, our life and our hearts and large chunks of our soul turned inside out. Everything changed. We rubbed our eyes and saw it clearly—we had a calling to go. Put shoes on, go where hurting people are, be their friends. It was the mother of all epiphanies."

It took eighteen months for their house to sell. Plenty of time to back out.

After living in a rental for a year, they moved their family into a rebuilding, declining neighborhood—with no assumptions or agendas. They were not trying to save anyone, they just moved in to live there. And here, among his people, in diversity, surrounded by poverty, God connects them with families. Shannan says, "I believe that God puts people in all our lives that he wants us to be in relationship with. He wants more than our casserole or our free baby-sitting. He wants us to fall in love with them."

Theirs are not the schools every mother and father dreams of for their children. When they got ready to move, they heard, "Okay, so you are committed to the move. But you are going to keep your kids here in this school (the *good* one), right?" Shannan admits that struggle:

> I understand the pull toward what feels most comfortable. I
> understand the deep desire to keep my children sheltered and

protected. But what I feel even stronger is the hope that my kids will learn very early that God goes with them. He goes. With them. Everywhere they are, there he is. I want them to be around kids who are like them and unlike them and every variation in between. I want them to see beauty in every face and to feel their faith grow as they relate to the world around them with each new day.

No agendas. Just obedience.

Essential trust. Essential grace.

And this is what it is, this life of dirty faith.

This is how we know what love is: Jesus Christ laid down his life for us. And we ought to lay down our lives for our brothers and sisters.

1 John 3:16

Acknowledgments

I spend a lot of time in this book talking about community, and to no small degree, community also describes the effort in putting the writing together. So many people played a role in calling the Church to a new commitment to the brothers and sisters of Jesus.

My heartfelt appreciation to:

Susan, not only my constant sojourner, but also my proofreader, my editor and re-writer, my constructive critic, and persistent cheerleader.

Philip and Corenne, Derli, and all the team at Hope Unlimited, for your heart, vision, and faithfulness to be the face of God for desperate children.

Andy McGuire and all the team at Bethany House, for your belief that these are words the Church needs to hear, for understanding that a title like *Dirty Faith* conveys a message, and for your support throughout the writing and publishing process.

Rickie, John, Burt, and Mimi for your willingness to be sounding boards, to engage and challenge ideas and concepts, and to encourage. And to Bill, Dot and Virgil, and Doris and Jackie for listening and responding.

Donna, for carving out time in my schedule to reflect and to write.

Stephen R. Carter at CleverSmith Writing for donating the *Dirty Faith* domain (dirtyfaith.com).

And most of all, to the children of Hope Unlimited who have embraced transformation and whose light has risen in the darkness.

Notes

Introduction

1. "12,000 Fewer Children Perish Daily in 2010 Than in 1990," UNICEF USA, September 15, 2011, http://www.unicefusa.org/news/releases/unicef-believes-in-zero.html.

2. Brook Larmer and Mac Margolis, "The Dead End Kids: Who Is Killing Brazil's Street Children?" *Newsweek*, May 25, 1992.

3. "Street Kids—The Facts," accessed April 6, 2014, http://www.streetkidsdirect.org.uk/index.php/street-kids-the-facts.

4. Donna Bowater, "Brazil Marks 20 Years Since Candelaria Child Massacre," *BBC News*, July 23, 2013, http://www.bbc.com/news/world-latin-america-23417669.

Chapter 1: Throwaway Kids and Peripheral People

1. U.S. Department of State—Bureau of Democracy, Human Rights, and Labor, "2009 Human Rights Report: Brazil," March 11, 2010, http://www.state.gov/j/drl/rls/hrrpt/2009/wha/136103.htm.

2. "12,000 Fewer Children Perish Daily in 2010 Than in 1990," UNICEF USA, September 15, 2011, http://www.unicefusa.org/news/releases/unicef-believes-in-zero.html.

3. "Child Protection From Violence, Exploitation, and Abuse," UNICEF, May 25, 2012, www.unicef.org/protection/57929_57999.html. Also,

"Juvenile Justice," International Catholic Child Bureau, www.bice.org/en/news/news/congress-2013-on-juvenile-justice.html.

4. David Barrett and Todd Johnson, *World Christian Trends AD 30–AD 2000* (Pasadena, CA.: William Carey Library, 2001), 363.

5. "Orphans," UNICEF, August 21, 2008, http://www.unicef.org/media/media_45279.html.

Chapter 2: Clay Vessels and Overflowing Hearts

1. C. S. Lewis, *Mere Christianity* (New York: HarperOne, 2001), 134.

Chapter 3: Seeking Relevance in a Post-Christian World

1. Ronald Sider, "The Scandal of the Evangelical Conscience," *Books and Culture*, January/February 2005, http://www.booksandculture.com/articles/2005/janfeb/3.8.html. Also, Larry Kreider and Floyd McClung, *Starting a House Church* (Ventura, CA: Regal Books, 2007), 107.

2. Claude Rosenberg and Tim Stone, "A New Take on Tithing," Stanford Social Innovation Review (Fall 2006), http://www.ssireview.org/articles/entry/a_new_take_on_tithing.

3. John Ronsvalle and Sylvia Ronsvalle, *The State of Church Giving Through 2004* (Champaign: empty tomb, inc., 2006), 1.

4. "Protestant Clergy and Laity Discuss Priorities for Spending Church Funds," Grey Matter Research and Consulting, May 10, 2006, www.greymatterresearch.com/index_files/Spending_Priorities.htm.

5. David Barrett, et al., *World Christian Trends, AD 30–AD 2200* (Pasadena, CA: William Carey Library, 2001), 520–529.

Chapter 4: Love Is the Final Apologetic

1. United States Central Intelligence Agency, *The World Factbook*, https://www.cia.gov/library/publications/the-world-factbook/rankorder/2119rank.html.

2. W. C. Martin, *Small Town, Big Miracle* (Carol Stream, IL: Tyndale House, 2007).

3. For more information on Calvary Chapel and its children's programs, visit www.4kidsofsfl.org.

Notes

Chapter 5: Tertiary Lives

1. Victims of Trafficking and Violence Protection Act of 2000, United States Public Law 106–386, October 28, 2000, http://www.state.gov/docu ments/organization/10492.pdf.

2. Cambodian National Council for Children, *Five Year Plan Against Sexual-Exploitation of Children 2000–2004* (March 17, 2000), http://www.protectionproject.org/wp-content/uploads/2010/11/NAP-Cambodia _2000-2004.pdf.

3. "Official: More Than 1M Child Prostitutes in India," CNN, May 11, 2009, http://edition.cnn.com/2009/WORLD/asiapcf/05/11/india.prostitu tion.children/.

4. Shasta Darlington, "Brazil Tackling Child Prostitution for World Cup," CNN, April 2, 2014, http://edition.cnn.com/2014/04/02/sport/foot ball/cfp-brazil-world-cup/index.html.

5. "Hope Unlimited Transforms Lives in Brazil," *NBC Nightly News*, January 5, 2007, http://www.nbcnews.com/id/16489053/ns/nbc_nightly_news _with_brian_williams-making_a_difference/t/hope-unlimited-transforms -lives-brazil/.

Chapter 6: In Prison, and You Visited Me

1. "DRC: Children Still in Prison Despite Law," *IRIN News*, June 29, 2011, http://www.irinnews.org/report/93100/drc-children-still-in-prison -despite-law.

2. Belkis Wille, "Young Behind Bars and Peril in Yemen," *Human Rights Watch*, March 7, 2013, www.hrw.org/news/2013/03/07young-behind -bars-and-peril-yemen.

3. Jessy Kaner, "The Colony for Russia's Young Offenders," *BBC Russian Service*, December 4, 2006, http://news.bbc.co.uk/2/hi/europe/ 6196362.stm.

4. United Nations Children's Fund, "Children in Detention: Calculating Global Estimates for Juvenile Justice Indicators 2 and 3," Program Division, UNICEF, New York, 2007 (internal document), reported in "Progress for Children," number 8, September 2009, http://www.unicef.org/ protection/files/Progress_for_Children-No.8_EN_081309%281%29.pdf.

Chapter 8: Dirty Faith on Dirt Paths

1. John 4:10–14

Chapter 10: A New Community

1. C. S. Lewis, *Mere Christianity* (New York: HarperOne, 2001), 134.
2. Ibid.

Chapter 11: Lives of Dirty Faith

1. Story adapted from http://orphansunday.org/about/.
2. Alene Snodgrass blogs about "stepping over fear to love a messy world" at Positively Alene (www.positivelyalene.com).
3. Shannan Martin blogs about her family's journey at Flower Patch Farmgirl (www.flowerpatchfarmgirl.com).

David Z. Nowell is an author, speaker, and the president of Hope Unlimited for Children. He and his wife, Susan, make their home in Jefferson City, Tennessee. Prior to joining Hope in 2007, he spent most of his career as a senior administrator at several Christian universities. He is a graduate of Baylor University with a PhD in historical theology. Nowell's blog, *Pursuing Dirty Faith*, encourages conversations about faith, orphan care, and lifestyle stewardship. Add your voice at www.davidznowell.com.